From Surviving to Thriving

*A Practical Guide to
Revitalize Your Church*

Rev. Dr. John H. Krahn

CSS Publishing Company, Inc.
Lima, Ohio

FROM SURVIVING TO THRIVING

Scripture quotations marked (RSV) are from the Revised Standard Version of the Bible, copyrighted 1946, 1952 ©, 1971, 1973, by the Division of Christian Education of the National Council of the Churches of Christ in the USA. Used by permission.

Library of Congress Cataloging-in-Publication Data

Names: Krahn, John H., 1943- author.
Title: From striving to thriving : a practical guide to revitalize your
  church / John H. Krahn.
Description: First [edition]. | Lima, OH : CSS Publishing Company, Inc.,
  2017. | Includes bibliographical references and index.
Identifiers: LCCN 2016052763 | ISBN 9780788028816 (pbk. : alk. paper)
Subjects: LCSH: Church renewal. | Non-church-affiliated people.
Classification: LCC BV600.3 .K74 2017 | DDC 253--dc23
LC record available at https://lccn.loc.gov/2016052763

For more information about CSS Publishing Company resources, visit our website at www.csspub.com, email us at csr@csspub.com, or call (800) 241-4056.

e-book:
ISBN-13: 978-0-7880-2882-3
ISBN-10: 0-7880-2882-0

ISBN-13: 978-0-7880-2881-6
ISBN-10: 0-7880-2881-2

PRINTED IN USA

Other Titles by John H. Krahn

Comments About This Book

"John Krahn cries out loudly for the church to reverse the downward trend in membership, worship, and giving. He calls for pastors and laity alike to remember whom they serve and the high calling of that service. He offers numerous practical ideas that will help church leaders turn their church around or keep a decline from ever occurring. Speaking from years of experience, Krahn is easy to read and understand. Persons doing so would be wise to put much of what they learn into practice."
Dr. J. Clif Christopher, United Methodist Clergy, and Author of *Not Your Parents' Offering Plate*

"The thing I like most about John Krahn's intervention into the downward spiral of a 'congregation at risk' is that he refuses to give in to rationalization and excuses for why the death of congregations is inevitable. Bonhoeffer has said, 'We must never be servile before the fact.' John starts with congregations where they are at and from within the situation walks with them in plain speech, practical ideas, and many years of pastoral wisdom. He understands that congregational renewal is about vision, and the church has no better vision than the Great Commission and the Great Commandment. Then he puts legs on this vision with chapters that encourage congregations to fix the money, get clear about worship, take concrete initiatives of mission, and invest in leadership. All of this comes with rich stories of lived parish experience. The chapters provide a road map of congregational renewal, with the end of each chapter containing ideas for implementation. Undergirding it all is a confidence in the power and presence of the crucified and risen Lord. This book is a gem."
Stephen Paul Bouman, Executive Director, Domestic Mission Unit of the ELCA

"Out of the ever-expanding literature on church transformation, Dr. Krahn has left his mark. His pastor's heart is revealed as he weaves his experience of renewal with the movement of church transformation. In these pages you will encounter many details around church renewal. Some of the details will be new and fresh,

while others will serve as reminders that will lead to more healthy churches. What I have appreciated the most about this book is his emphasis on the Holy Spirit in the process of renewal."
Ray Jones, Associate Director of Evangelism, Presbyterian Church (USA)

"In this delightfully practical and inspiring book, Dr. Krahn appeals to all who love Jesus and understand the centrality of the congregation in our life as disciples, to raise our game. Krahn understands excellence as the goal in all that we do in the name of Jesus, even as grace and unconditional acceptance are the message. Krahn unapologetically pairs the theological with the prudent and exchanges nostalgia with an unwavering trust in the work of the Holy Spirit today. Read this book to move from a focus on congregational survival to offering a thriving witness to God's love and grace."
Christina Jackson-Skelton, ELCA Executive Director, Mission Advancement

"John Krahn draws on a half-century of experience in ordained ministry to provide encouragement to congregations that are struggling in a changing religious landscape. Both clergy and lay leaders will find useful and practical ideas for bringing new energy to their congregations. More than anything else, however, this little book is an antidote to the despair that has infected so many congregations who are weighed down by declining numbers, changing neighborhoods, and decaying buildings. The solutions may not be easy, and the changes needed may be unsettling, but Krahn articulates what we know deep inside: the power behind us is greater than the task ahead of us."
The Reverend Canon William C. Parnell, Canon to the Ordinary, Episcopal Diocese of Massachusetts

"Reverend Dr. John Krahn is a leader with infectious hope for the renewal of the church. Through engaging storytelling and personal reflection on his 50-year journey as an ordained leader in the Lutheran church, Dr. Krahn shares assessable, real-life strategies to help struggling congregations refashion and reclaim a life and

a future. *From Surviving to Thriving: A Practical Guide to Revitalize Your Church* looks honestly at the significant shift that has taken place in American culture regarding religiosity and participation in faith communities. With honest eyes and an authentic approach, Dr. Krahn provides a message of hope in challenging times. I highly recommend this book. It contains a word of hope just when we need to hear one!"
Rev. J. Elise Brown, PhD, Kairos and Associates, Inc.

"John Krahn has put together counsel for those churches that need and are ready to do the tasks required to invigorate a viable and vital congregation. Getting started is the first task, staying engaged is the second, and the third is making use of Krahn's insight and challenge."
Dr. Peter Steinke, Congregations Systems Consultant, Author of *Teaching Fish to Walk*

Dedication

This book is dedicated to the clergy and laypeople who work hard to welcome people into a saving faith in our Lord Jesus Christ and to make their church a vital expression of God's love for the world both in words and deeds.

Table of Contents

Foreword

You will find in this book *From Surviving to Thriving* by Reverend Dr. John H. Krahn — a good measure of practical advice, pressed down, shaken together, and running over with experience and good sense. There are not many suggestions in this book that cannot immediately be put into practice by pastors and members of congregations alike.

Pastor Krahn has done what he recommends and has seen the results of intentional missional ministry in more than one context. The book is overflowing with good stories and examples of excellent ministry. He draws richly from the pastoral imagination of other settings.

We all know that the current culture does not necessarily support our congregational revitalization, but rather than simply analyze the situation and describe the problem, the author proposes concrete and effective practices in worship, finance, and programs that he has seen work. Our Christian mission and ministry is highly adaptable and, throughout history and the world, has regularly thrived at times and places where the context is hostile or resistant.

There are no silver bullets to address our challenges but a comprehensive approach includes, among other actions, getting the church's financial house in order, practicing good stewardship, developing a strategic plan and vision, marketing the church in new and old ways, and developing an evangelism program. Here is a book by a veteran pastor who knows how to revitalize a congregation that is long on hope and short on excuses.

Since retiring from the presidency of the seminary, I have become the interim pastor of a wonderful congregation that was experiencing all of the challenges of the contemporary context: declining worship attendance and financial resources and the attendant frustrations of building debt and depleting resources. I am pleased to say that in regular conversations with the author of this book and using some of his ideas, the 150-year-old parish is now more than $10,000 ahead of budget, and we have received about thirty new members in the past twelve months. Worship attendance is up by 20%, and God has given us a spirit of confidence and hope. By God's grace, it is amazing what the ideas in this book can accomplish.

I want to publicly thank the author for writing this useful book. So many of our churches do not need to cocoon or close. With fervent prayer and hard work along with bold initiatives, these churches can be revitalized. *From Surviving to Thriving: A Practical Guide to Revitalize Your Church* can help lead the way.

Dr. Philip Krey, former president of LutheranTheological Seminary in Philadelphia and ELCA pastor

Introduction

Is your church weaker than it was ten years ago or even five years ago? On Sunday morning are the pews in your church rarely full? Do you have more people in your church over sixty than under sixty? Is balancing your church's budget something that is an anxious struggle most every year? If you answered *yes* to any of these questions, then I have written this book especially for you. Unfortunately, many of our churches in every denomination are stressed. Nearly a third are struggling to just survive, and record numbers are actually closing.

If you are a concerned member of a struggling church, *From Surviving to Thriving: A Practical Guide to Revitalize Your Church* is for you. If you are a leader, be it a member of your church's elected leadership group or your church's stewardship or evangelism committee, then this book is a must for you. If you are a minister of a church merely surviving, then you will need to read this book. In it you will discover many practical and proven ideas to revitalize your church's ministry.

Because I have helped failing churches for nearly fifty years, this book presents practical suggestions for your church that have been proven over my many years in ministry. Each chapter also concludes with insightful "Action Items" that will promote meaningful discussion on how to put what is learned into practice.

My entire ministry serving multiple churches as both pastor and interim pastor has been with churches that were in decline. I was even sent to some of these churches and was instructed to hold their hands until they died. Church officials had given up on them and saw them closing. Not one of them did, and every one of them is still bringing people to Jesus Christ in the communities they serve. The power of prayer and the Holy Spirit, when used with good practices, can turn any church around. This book not only tells how to do this, but it also tells the exciting stories of our God still performing Pentecost-like miracles today.

If you have read this far and your church is bucking the trend and is in great shape, you will find additional ideas in this book that will be useful for your ministry as well. You too will benefit from reading it. I have always been interested in learning from successful churches. In this book, I have included many things that I have learned from them.

In conclusion, I wish to thank the members of each church that I have served who have helped to educate me over the years. Every church, be it the largest Lutheran church in New York or a tiny struggling multiracial church in a poor community, has helped inform many of my recommendations covered in this book. I wish to thank my colleague in ministry, Winston Dookram, who encouraged me to write this book. I also would like to thank my wife, Doris, along with JoAnn Breitbach and Evelyn Andersen Meyers for doing a careful job of proofreading and making thoughtful suggestions that have improved it.

One

Stop Making Excuses and
Start Doing Something

As a child, Larry Walters always dreamed of flying. He was fascinated with flight. As soon as he was old enough, he signed up for the Air Force. "Off we go into the wild blue yonder...." Much to his chagrin, his eyes were weak, and he was not allowed into flight school. But the dream never left him.

Years later, as he sat in his lawn chair in his backyard in the Los Angeles area, an idea popped into his mind. What if he tied helium-filled balloons to his lawn chair and floated off into the sky? What a wonderful thought. He hurried down to the local Army Navy store and purchased 45 big, sturdy weather balloons. He purchased helium tanks from California Toy Time Balloons. Back home he made himself a few sandwiches, and with them he packed a beer into a picnic bag. Then he grabbed his son's BB gun. Pretty soon all of the balloons were inflated. The lawn chair was tied to the bumper of his truck. Larry put on a parachute, sat in the chair, gun and picnic lunch in his lap, and cut loose the chair.

His plan was to float gently above the trees for a few hours, have something to eat, and then with the BB gun shoot several balloons until he floated lazily back to earth. But it did not go as planned. When he cut the cord tied to his truck, he shot up into the air like a bullet to 15,000 feet before leveling off at about 8,000 feet. Initially he was afraid to use his BB gun to shoot any of the balloons for fear that the chair would become unstable, and he would fall out.

So there he was floating helplessly. The winds started to blow him into the flight corridor of Long Beach airport.

The story goes that a pilot saw him and radioed to the tower, "There is a man tethered to some balloons up here sitting in a lawn chair with a rifle in his lap." What I would have given to see the face of the flight controller.

After 45 minutes in the sky, Larry shot out several balloons before dropping his son's BB gun overboard. He descended slowly and safely to the ground, but the balloon cables became caught in a power line and caused a twenty-minute power outage in a Long Beach neighborhood. The news media, having picked up the story, swarmed him as he was being led away by the police. "Larry why did you do it?" one reporter shouted at him. Larry's answer was, "It was something I had to do."

The church is in tough shape today. Some studies suggest that upward of 90% of all churches are either declining in membership or have plateaued. In my denomination, in the synod to which I belong, 40% of all the churches cannot afford a full-time pastor. A total of fifty congregations close every week in the USA, which becomes a staggering 2,600 per year. One could argue that in a little more than a lifetime the church, as we know it today, may no longer exist. This is no time to just sit around. There is much we have to do.

The median number of worshipers for all denominations combined is 75 people on a Sunday morning. This means that half of all congregations are worshiping 75 or less per week. Usually this is barely enough people to support a pastor and keep the doors open. On the average Sunday, only 18% of the population in the USA attends church. I preach at a lot of different churches as a supply pastor. Usually two thirds of the people I see at worship are seventy or older. If something doesn't change, one does not need to be overly astute to see the bleakness of the future for the church.

It is also true that the older a church gets, the less it grows. Newly planted churches increase rapidly. Why? There are several reasons. They need to grow in order to exist. Church mission boards fund them for only a few years pushing them to grow and meet their expenses on their own. Often they attract a younger, more energetic congregation. People cannot say, "Ask someone else, I've already done that." Starting a new congregation is inherently exciting as you give it birth.

The current state of the church, quite understandably, can leave pastors and church leaders feeling defeated. In the fifties on Long Island, where I currently live, there could be ten churches with ten pastors that from the least effective to the go-getter, would all grow. Today, only one is growing. The other nine are dying. The church is a living organism. It is either growing, or it is dying. In the church I first served out of seminary, the head pastor, just before he took a call to Florida, looked at his declining congregation and said, "It is like putting my hand under a faucet with the water rushing through my fingers, and I cannot grab it."

With all of the negativity out there and the statistics I have just outlined, it is quite understandable that pastors and church leaders often sit around and have a pity party. Excuses for failure also abound. I hear them all the time.

"There are three Lutheran churches within a mile of our church."

"My community is now 25% Asian."

"So many of our good, active members have died or moved away."

"People are no longer as committed as they used to be."

I have heard these same excuses for nearly fifty years. In a ten-mile radius of most churches, there is a great mission field of unchurched people. There is a plethora of people who need your church. Negative thinking only weakens your efforts.

I was supply preaching at a dying congregation in a community heavily populated with Jewish people. A new, beautiful, large Jewish center had just been built across the street from this little church. People told me, "We can't grow, there are only Jewish people living around our church." It was around Christmas, and I noticed that at least one out of three homes on the block in which this church was located had Christmas lights decorating their property. I pointed this out to the church's leaders and suggested that they walk through their community listing all of the addresses of the homes with lights and evangelize these neighbors throughout the coming year.

Great Commission or Great Omission?

In many moderate to liberal denominations, the Great Commission has become the great omission. Before Christ ascended into heaven, he gave his followers the imperative to go and make disciples of all nations. It was not an optional activity. The church's mission is to know Christ and to make Christ known. It is easy to understand why moderate to liberal denominations are declining more than 5% each year. Sharing Jesus Christ in the power of the Holy Spirit and leading the lost to the Lord are no longer the top priority of many of these denominations. Evangelical churches that are sharing Christ and teaching their members how to disciple others are growing in spite of the negative cultural influences of our day. Excuses have been replaced with energetic and creative witnessing.

In 1 Peter 2:9-10, we read (RSV):

> *But you are a chosen race, a royal priesthood, a holy nation, God's own people, that you may declare the wonderful deeds of him who called you out of darkness into his marvelous light. Once you were no people but now you are God's people; once you had not received mercy but now you have received mercy.*

Through God's mercy, which has made us God's own people, we have been called to give witness to the wonderful deeds of God to the communities in which God has planted us. The entire church is called to be a witnessing community, both through its shared witness as well as the witness of each individual member. Thus it is the church's and every individual Christian's mission to take the gospel into the home, into the community, and into the entire world. Not only did Peter and Paul and the apostles believe and write about this, their life's work testified to it. Ultimately they gave their lives for declaring the love of God through Jesus Christ.

In Matthew 16:18, we read (RSV), "And I tell you, you are Peter, and on this rock I will build my church, and the powers of death shall not prevail against it." God assures us that the church will never perish, but your individual church just might. I have read some authors who hide behind this verse to say that the church will somehow survive. The implication is that we should not be so concerned by the current condition of things. The church, throughout its history, has had its ups and downs. This is true, but this does not give us cover for being unfaithful in proclaiming the good news of salvation to everyone in earshot and welcoming the lost into our churches. Only about one third of the world's population is Christian. We have our work cut out for us. In my denomination, we have become quite good at closing churches. Some pastors have developed a ministry to terminally ill congregations. I call them church hospice care pastors. We even have a liturgical rite when we close a church. A diagnostic tool has also been developed to help determine when a church should be closed. Unfortunately, I do not know of a program that has been developed pointing out the steps needed to keep a church open. When we expect a church to close, we are inclined to live up to that expectation. Nowhere in scripture do I find this kind of thinking. Yes, I guess there may be a circumstance when a church must close. The last two that I have pastored were deemed to be on life support.

Both were candidates for church hospice care. Both are now alive and well. It can be done.

In the synod to which I belong, only about one third of the financial support to fund the synod's ministry comes from donations by its 192 congregations. That's how financially weak many of our churches currently are. Most of the other money needed comes from the sale of churches that close. If the money from the sale of church property dried up, staff would be laid off and mission work lessened. We would find ourselves in a terrible bind. When the last congregation is sold, soon thereafter all church work would cease. The answer to this dilemma is to revitalize the 192 congregations to the point that they can also once again totally support the work of the synod and the church at large.

"It was something I had to do," as our friend Larry Walters proclaimed. We all need to get out of our ruts and start doing something. No one is saying that it is going to be easy. This book presents much of what I have learned in nearly fifty years of ordained ministry. I have been called to serve dying churches my entire career. I recently told an assistant to my bishop, "It is not in my DNA to close churches." With God's help, no church that I have served has closed under my watch. With God's help, I left every one stronger than I found it.

In the first congregation that I served nearly fifty years ago, I had been called as "Assistant to the Pastor." About four years into the call, the head pastor left, and I was asked to be the head pastor of the parish. At that time, it was still the largest Lutheran church in New York. My father advised me to not accept the call, for this church had been in decline for nearly a decade. My dad said, "You are a young man. You should be energetically starting a new church. The church you are now serving is dying. Let someone older become its pastor." In many ways he was right, but I felt that trying to turn this church around needed all of the energy and panache of a younger man, so I took the call.

Nearly Every Church Needs Revitalization

Your church does not need to be in intensive care to require revitalization. The Holy Spirit has the power to renew any church in whatever shape it currently finds itself. There is also genuine excitement and joy in being in a church that God has in the crosshairs for revitalization. When things have gone south, and you can see that your talents are not enough to effect the change needed, this is the time you call out to God in prayer and give God room to do a miracle.

In my denomination, there seems to be a great deal of effort put forth in trying to combine two failing congregations. Sometimes one is sold, and the people and proceeds from the sale join with a geographically close and somewhat stronger congregation. This is lifted up with much fanfare as a wonderful thing. There are some benefits, I admit, but for the most part, I do not get it. If two parishes join together and the people in both average seventy years old, this gives us one congregation slightly bigger but still with an old, soon to be dying, group of people. Unless the money gained from the sale of one of the churches is used to help the "new" congregation more effectively reach the community for Christ, then little has been accomplished for the long term.

Friends, the first step in solving a problem is to admit that you have one. "Hello, my name is John, and I serve a dying church." Six months ago, I received a call from the bishop's assistant asking if I would consider becoming the interim pastor of another congregation that was dying. The pastors of neighboring Lutheran churches who knew this church, told me that they felt it would not survive. The bishop also told me that this was unfortunately his opinion as well.

On my first Sunday in this parish, I informed the congregation that it had a projected deficit of $46,000 by the end of its fiscal year with only $20,000 in the bank to cover it. "If things stay this way, in about five months, around Easter, we will run out of money and have to close our church," I announced. The people looked shocked. This was the first time anyone boldly laid out the problem for them. But this is the first step needed in any turnaround; you must let the people know in exact, concrete terms the extent of the problem you are facing together with no sugar coating allowed.

This book will tell their story as well as the story of other churches God has saved and revitalized. It will show both pastors and lay leaders numerous ways to strengthen their parishes and move them from surviving to thriving. In case you might be wondering, the parish I currently serve was worshiping an average of fifty people six months ago. Today it averages 75. Weekly offerings averaged $1,440 from January to November before I arrived. Now the average weekly offering is $3,200. In November it had a projected deficit of $46,000. Now we are projecting a *surplus* of over $170,000.

A lot of prayer and hard work have gone into this turnaround. Nothing worthwhile is ever accomplished without fervent prayer and hard work. Some of you may be thinking, "I am too old to do this; I am past my prime." I am officially retired and 71 years old. Remember God also called Abraham after he had received the gold watch. Stop making excuses and start working. In this book, we will consider many practical things both pastors and lay leaders can do to help revitalize their churches.

Develop a Dynamic Mission and Vision Statement

Here is the best place to begin. Develop a dynamic mission and vision statement for your ministry. You need to state clearly and concisely why your church exists and what it hopes to accomplish. Whenever I go into a deli, I go for ham and potato salad. I expect the store to have it and want to sell me as much of it as possible. When I go into an auto supply store, I expect it to have windshield wiper blades. I do not expect wiper blades to be in a deli or ham and potato salad to be found in my auto supply store. Each has its primary purpose. The primary mission of the church is to share the gospel with those both inside and outside its physical walls and to assist those who accept the Lord lead a God-pleasing life before going to heaven. Its primary vision is to lead others to Christ. It does this in every way possible that it can find. This is not the only mission of the church, but it must be primary.

The church is also called to address issues of social and economic justice and to help overcome various kinds of oppression. It is to be a force to effect the betterment of the world. Feeding the hungry, standing up for the weak, providing for the sick and being the compassionate presence of Christ is our calling as well. But as our numbers become less and as we close churches, our ability to perform this aspect of our mission becomes less as well. It only stands to reason that when we do a better job of reaching more people for the Lord and having them join our ranks, we will also become a more effective force for good in our world.

A Christian business owner said that when he interviews a new employee he asks, "What is your purpose in life?" He then sits back and watches the prospective employee stutter and stammer trying to answer this unexpected question. He was delightfully surprised when one man answered without hesitation, "to get to heaven and to bring as many people with me as possible." Shouldn't this be every Christian's and church's primary mission?

Churches without this as their primary goal, even if they survive, will not thrive. I am sorry that I do not find this mission and vision front and center in my own denomination. It is an aspect of what we do, but it does not appear to be our primary mission and vision. Tell people that your church is the place where they can be loved by God. It is the place where they will find the saving grace of Christ crucified and risen. Through your church, they will receive forgiveness and be assured of an eternal future. Invite them into your church family so that they can also become part of God's forever family.

With your mission and vision clearly stated, look at everything you are currently doing in your church and ask the questions, "Why are we doing this?" "What is its purpose?" "Does it advance our mission and help us attain our vision?" "Are we providing services for our people they could just as easily attain elsewhere?" These nice things you may be doing are not bad, but they take away the resources of time, money and energy from the more important things you should be doing.

Many pastors run wonderful programs for seniors, singles, or other smaller groups in the church. They plan for speakers and other activities. The pastor often becomes a committee of one who does nearly all of the work. Is this the best use of the pastor's time to advance the kingdom? I doubt it. These groups are more than capable of conducting their own program once the pastor helps to get them organized and running. By handing over the program to the participants to run, the pastor will have more time to witness to the unchurched in the community.

Giving up the good for the better will be hard. You will receive some pushback from your parishioners. Be courageous, and remember for whom you are working. Pleasing God and witnessing about God's love and salvation to those inside of your church, as well as those outside of your church, must always be your first priority.

Action Items

1) Counteract any negative, defeatist thinking in your church, replacing it with the possibilities and promises that God presents.

2) Implement ways in which your church can better carry out the Great Commission in your community and the world.

3) Consider ways your church can benefit from revitalization.

4) Take the first step and make your church aware of the major problems you are currently facing.

5) Put the sharing of Christ crucified and risen at the center of your church's mission and vision statement.

6) Ask of everything you are currently doing in your church, "Does this activity or program advance our mission and help us fulfill our vision?" Stop doing what does not.

Two

Get Your Church's
Financial House in Order

At the first church I served right out of the seminary, the head pastor, Edward H. Stammel, was a self-taught and excellent fund-raiser. He personally led a number of successful capital campaigns for our church as well as for the church at large. In one building renovation of our church, the front of the church was completely redone in order to receive an exact replica of Lorenzo Ghiberti's world-famous bronze doors, the Gates of Paradise. These huge gates leading into our church were donated by one parishioner in memory of his recently deceased wife and son. They were also covered in 24-carat gold leaf, and the church became known as the church with the golden doors. These gates were so impressive that a picture of them was featured on the cover of our national church's *Annual Yearbook* which listed all of its churches and clergy in the USA.

That same year Pastor Stammel was invited to talk to seminarians of the church on the subject of stewardship. One of my later assistant pastors had been present at his lecture. He told me that before hearing him, he and most of the students saw him as the pastor none of them wished to emulate... the guy whose church had golden doors. He then related Stammel's talk. Knowing some of the students' sentiments, Stammel began his memorable talk this way. "I love money." "I love money." "I looove money!" As he said these words, he rubbed his hands together like a greedy miser. The students were appalled. But he had captured their attention. He then told them that he did not love money for money's sake, but that it helped him to be able to share the gospel, to feed the poor, to help the outcast in society, and to support the church's mission of making Christ known throughout the world.

It is amazing to me how many clergy and lay leaders see both talking about and asking for money as something distasteful. Money in and of itself is not evil. It is only evil when we make obtaining it the first priority in our lives. When you choose to work and miss church for the sake of obtaining more money, then there is a problem. It is when the love of money forces God to take a backseat in your life that it is bad. Money in and of itself is needed by the church to carry out Christ's mission in the world. Jesus spent much of his teaching centered on money and generous giving. He was never embarrassed speaking about it; neither should we be.

As a young seminarian, I was leading worship for the first time in my home parish. Prior to the service my parish pastor was leading me through the steps, and at one point forgot to mention the place in the service where we took the offering. I smartly said, "Lutherans would never miss an opportunity to take an offering." He brought me up short by saying, "We wouldn't, because it is an important part of our worship." Giving and giving generously are acts of worship.

A former bishop of mine, The Reverend Dr. William Lazareth, once said in a sermon, "Show me your checkbook, and I will show you your God." We spend our money on what is important to us. Cars are not important to me. I nurse mine along for ten years or more. Travel is, so I spend a good deal of money on vacations. God and the church are most important to me, so I contribute 20% of my income to the Lord.

Most churches are struggling financially. Some pastors nearing retirement are just praying that their churches do not run out of money before they retire. Many churches are greatly underpaying their pastors. When their pastor retires, they sadly discover that they were paying him/her less than the denominational salary guidelines for a new pastor right out of the seminary.

Some congregations, who have received legacies, are spending this money down in order to balance their budgets every year. Other churches with vacant parsonages sell them just to remain afloat. Having received a generous bequest, the church I am currently serving had $300,000 in the bank ten years ago. It spent it down $30,000 a year until it nearly closed.

A former mentor of mine told me early in my career, "There are only two ways to balance a budget... spend less money and raise more money." It is as simple and as hard as spending less while raising more. In order to get your church's financial house in order, first you need to discover how you can spend less of God's money. I am not suggesting that you cut out any of your ministry. I am suggesting that you do everything you are presently doing but do it more cost effectively. I have made it a practice that before asking a congregation to give one more dime to the church, I would first make sure that we are spending their offerings in the most efficient manner possible. When people see all of our efforts to spend their offerings more wisely, they are then more willing to respond positively when asked to give more. Getting your financial house in order is the first thing you need to work on in revitalizing your church. You need to be able to pay the bills first and buy time to be able to work on all the rest.

Some Ways to Save the
Lord's Money

You really need to visit every line in your budget, and ask yourself whether there are some savings that might be affected. Let me share with you some amazing things that I have found in churches I have served. One church had nine refrigerators. Some were completely empty or held only a quart of spoiled milk. We got rid of four of them. This was money saved. In this same church we cut the cost on phone service by 30%, for we were under an old plan that was much more expensive. I discovered that every month we were also paying for a phone line that we no longer used. We canceled it.

In another church we were paying nearly $200 a year in fees for telephones we were supposedly renting. No one had seen these phones in years, but the church treasurer faithfully paid the bill every year. I figured that this church wasted over $2,000 of the Lord's money on this omission alone.

Here is a good way to cut the cost of your church offering envelopes. In the church I am now serving, one of my parishioners came up with an idea that cut the cost of our church offering envelopes more than half. Last year we spent $1,200 on traditional numbered packets of envelopes. This year we spent $500, less than half resulting in a $700 savings. We now are using standard 3 1/2 by 6 1/2-inch envelopes, and we have them printed locally. On the front is the name and address of the church. There are lines in the upper left-hand corner for the name and return address of the giver. In the right-hand corner is a little square where the stamp is affixed. Written in the square is "Place Stamp Here or Return in Offering Plate." On the left side of the envelope is a little line art of the three crosses of Calvary.

We packed 52 in a larger envelope along with a letter explaining that when a parishioner had to miss church, it was important to mail in the offering that week. Our new offering envelopes are all ready to be mailed. We track people's offering by name. Most place their names on the envelope. Those who do not most often donate by check, so we put their names on their envelope for them. It works very well. We put the amount given also on each envelope and then record the donation in our computer program, which will eventually print out giving statements.

We have extra packets of our generic envelopes in the narthex and have a note in the weekly bulletin encouraging those without envelopes to take one of the packets. Nearly every week someone takes a packet. For special services like Good Friday, we mail an additional envelope with the letter encouraging worship at the special service. These we hand code with a little red "F" in the lower left-hand corner since we track the amount of giving at special services. Unused envelopes from one year are used the next year. There is no waste this way.

We tell our people that we need their offering for all 52 weeks. At the end of the year, there should not be one envelope left in their packets. We periodically remind our people how many envelopes they should have used by a certain date. The second Sunday in June we declare "Snow Sunday." On this Sunday we especially encourage our people to send in the envelopes and offerings they may have missed during the winter due to inclement weather. In the late fall we declare "Vacation Sunday," using the same idea.

Bulletins are another source for potential savings. Most churches that I have visited (there have been very many) print too many bulletins. The church will not collapse should it occasionally run out of bulletins. Actually, it can be a good thing, for it says that more people than expected attended worship that Sunday. There is also nothing wrong with giving people a chance to practice the Christian virtue of sharing their bulletin with the person sitting next to them. Every week I try to anticipate the number of worshipers for the following Sunday and then decide the number of bulletins to print. This cuts the cost of printing and paper considerably.

Electric bills can easily be lessened. Remove energy-guzzling appliances. Only turn on lights when you need them. In two churches that I served, the head usher arrived an hour before the first service began — good so far. The first thing the usher did was turn on all of the lights in the church. In one of the churches I served, an electrician calculated that the cost of lighting the church for one hour was $25 or more. The first worshiper arrived less than thirty minutes before the service began. I instructed the usher not to turn on the church lights until the first worshiper arrived. This saved the church $12.50 per week. Not a whole lot but in a year's time the savings came to $650. Turning off the lights as soon as the last person left added more savings.

All lightbulbs in your church should be changed into compact fluorescent bulbs or LED bulbs. Yes, they cost more. So what if you do not have the money for the initial outlay? Let your people know that you need so many bulbs at a cost of so much, and ask them to help you save on the electric cost by buying one or more bulbs. Tell them also the total cost of replacing every bulb in the church building and any other buildings you have as well. Someone who believes strongly in saving our planet may well spring for the whole amount. Replacing components in old fluorescent fixtures brings even more savings.

You might also want to consider adding solar panels for the greatest savings on your electricity bill. My home church did not have money to install solar energy. Nevertheless, since several members were interested, we pursued this option. In the end, just five families donated the $100,000 plus needed to install the solar panels. We are now saving $17,000 a year in electrical costs. Never assume that there is no money for anything worthwhile that you wish to do. First pray, then ask.

I have often felt that the churches I have served must have stock in the local oil or gas company. During the coldest days of winter, parishioners often leave the entrance doors to the church's buildings wide open. I see dollar bills escaping into the cold. Year round on Sundays some churches believe in keeping the church doors open to indicate to the community that their church is welcoming everyone to enter. Observing this behavior in the dead of winter, I wonder how many people from the community think, "Are these people nuts?"

Everything is negotiable. Please embrace this important concept, and your church will save money. Speak to every vendor and ask for a better price than you are now getting. The worst that will happen is that they will say "no." Not one of them will raise your price because you asked. Recently a plumber charged $900 for needed repair work. I called the owner of the plumbing company and told him how strapped the church was for funds. I then asked him if he could cut the bill in half. He told me that this was not possible, but he did reduce the price to $600. We do not have one $300-a-week giver, however that was the savings added to our ministry that week. Our snow removal company also halved the price it had been charging us. A $1,000 savings resulted. Each conversation took just five minutes.

At another church, I acquired competitive bids on our garbage collection and reduced our cost also by half. That saving was $1,400. Permit me just one more of many examples from my ministry. An attorney we contracted was charging my current church $400 per hour. The final bill for his services was over $4,000. Because of tight finances, we made our case and requested a reduction. He gave us a courtesy discount of $3,000. This equaled a week's offering. Be creative. Be bold. You are asking on behalf of the Lord and the ministry of the church.

Two other areas to cut expenses significantly are the cost of a copy machine rental and church insurance. Rent or buy a copy machine just big enough to meet your basic needs. Forget the bells and whistles. You have several retired people in your church who would be happy to collate your Sunday bulletins each week. No need to pay more for a copier that does this for you. There are dozens of companies that want your business. Play "Let's Make a Deal" with them all. Start this process at least six months before your present contract expires. Do not jump at the first offer. Let's say you are now paying $2,000 a year; ask each vendor what it can provide you for $1,000 a year, which will meet your needs.

Insurance is a big, big expense item. At the congregation I currently serve, the cost was $21,000 a year. We cut it by 25% by assuming more risk and cutting out some elements of coverage. For example, we are no longer covered if our facilities are destroyed by a terrorist attack. We figured that Syosset, New York, was not very high on any terrorist's hit list. Removing this saved us money. We were in such difficult financial straits, we felt there was more risk to our church's survival by not cutting our insurance coverage. This high expense was one of the main factors contributing to our possible demise. Less insurance and money saved better ensured our survival. Now that we have turned the corner and are in good shape financially, we will add back some of the coverage we needed to forego.

In the church I am presently serving, we unfortunately needed to cut the salaries of the entire staff by a minimum of 10%. There are twelve paid staff. All but three are teachers in our nursery school. Some of our staff we needed to cut as much as 40%. Had we not done this, we would have closed. We met with our staff several times prior to making the cuts explaining why this was necessary. No one quit after the cuts took place.

Ways to Increase Your Church's Income
There are many excellent books and resources to increase the financial stewardship of your parish. Every denomination has multiple resources and programs available to its churches. If you are willing to read just one book on stewardship, I would recommend *Not Your Parent's Offering Plate*, by J.

Clif Christopher. It is one of the most impressive and stimulating books I have read on the subject. It can be a game changer for your ministry and your parish.

The basic rule for getting more income for your parish is quite simple: You need to ask for it. But before doing that there is something else, other than cutting expenses, you must do. I started in my present parish a month before Christmas. I began my ministry there by calling every family of the parish on the telephone. I disciplined myself to make ten calls per day, and in about fifteen days I called everyone. For those I could not reach, I left a message on their voice mail. I told everyone frankly that we were facing a $46,000 deficit and had only enough resources left to remain open until about Easter. I asked them to do two things: Pray daily for their church and join us for worship the following Sunday. I told them that things were so bad, there wasn't even enough money to pay me as their interim pastor or my colleague serving as a vicar.

I have a vicar assisting me. A vicar in my denomination is a seminary intern who works under a pastor as part of his/her practical training before ordination. Vicar Winston Dookram is a seventy-year-old, second career insurance executive who is only six months my junior. I affectionately referred to him as "The Kid." As I said, neither of us is being paid for our ministry. At this stage of our lives, we are both fortunate to be sufficiently blessed to be able to do this. He has been a partner and blessing to this congregation as well. Having a vacancy for nearly two years, they now have more than the full-time pastor they need.

Because of the telephone calls, more people came to worship, and our offerings increased. We also launched the power of concentrated daily prayer. Every week at the end of our service, we have a "Moment of Mission" when I bring everyone up-to-date on the cuts made and the cost-effective savings we have put into place. Around Christmas, I asked them to consider giving 100% of their end of the year charitable giving to our church at the expense of other worthy charities that they normally supported. I told the congregation that the other charities would most likely be around at the end of the New Year, but this church might not. This request increased our giving as well.

In the New Year, I launched our small group, stewardship effort. I cleared my schedule and set up multiple, one-hour meetings several times a week. Over the month I had more than twenty meetings. The vicar conducted a few meetings as well. I scheduled three families at a time to meet with me to discuss their involvement in ensuring the future of their church. It is a fact that the smaller the group, the more effective the meeting, and the greater the result. The best result would have come from meeting with each family individually. But time for this was not on our side. Easter was not that far away

Each meeting began with prayer. I asked every family what their church meant to them, and why it was important to them that it continued. I talked about the importance of prayer and regular worship and our need to commit to both. Then I told them the story of one elderly woman's response to one of the 150 telephone calls I made. During our conversation she said, "I won't let Faith close." This blew me away. I did not question what she was willing to do. I took her at her word. Here was someone with the commitment we needed to go forward. I told everyone at the meeting that the more people were willing to join this woman in her strong commitment to the Lord's church, the likelihood of the church closing would be avoided.

I also witnessed to the people gathered about tithing and how I am personally blessed as a tither. Tithing is giving 10% of your income to the Lord. The inevitable question arose whether the tithe should be upon one's gross or net income. I always respond to this question by answering, "It depends on how much you want to be blessed." Look at the last book in the Old Testament and read Malachi 3:10 (RSV). It says, "Bring the full tithes into the storehouse, that there may be food in my house; and thereby put me to the test, says the Lord of hosts, if I will not open the windows of heaven for you and pour down for you an overflowing blessing." This makes the case quite well for tithing. I invited those present to join me and become tithers. Since most people were unwilling to become tithers all at once, I asked them to work towards tithing by committing more of their income to the Lord in addition to their current giving. They were encouraged to do this each year until they became tithers.

I also talked about remembering the church in their will. By tithing of their estate, they would witness to their children of their love for the Lord. They would also help strengthen Christ's ministry beyond their lives.

On the back of the commitment sheet, I asked them to write any additional thoughts or questions they might wish to share with me. We then went into the church, and I prayed that God would direct their decisions. They completed their commitment form, put it in an envelope on which they had earlier written their name and address, and placed it into a basket on the church altar. The following Sunday we had a prayer of blessing on their commitments and dedicated them and their generosity to the Lord. After I made a copy for our records, each person's original commitment was mailed back to him/her along with a letter of thanks for meeting with me.

The results were impressive. Nearly everyone pledged daily prayer for the church, weekly worship, a commitment to do what it takes so that the church would not close, and an increase in giving... some dramatically. Eight families said that they already had the church in their wills or would now include it in their wills. From this point, our offerings and attendance took off. Attendance increased by 25%, and our offerings more than doubled. It was clear that God was powerfully at work in this congregation.

I know that there are many good stewardship programs available for you to embrace. You should not do the same one year after year. But the pastor willing to meet an hour with each family in his/her congregation should have excellent results. In the case of my present congregation, we could not afford to do less.

One more thing: be bold in asking for what you need. I once had to help a local Lutheran high school from going bankrupt because of bad management. It needed $400,000 in hand within three months to just keep the doors open. No bank would lend the school a dime. I first met with a dozen people with the ability of giving $5,000 and up. When I asked each one for a specific amount, I told them that we needed exactly that much or more. "Do not give us less, because we won't be able to remain open, and your gift will be lost." Not one person turned me down. I was not asking for myself. I was asking for the Lord and to save one of God's important ministries. Boldness in the Lord's service is often needed.

Permit me at this point to address one of my pet peeves. Over the years many whom I asked to increase their commitment to the Lord gave me this excuse: "But pastor, I am retired now and am on a fixed income. I cannot help." Really? In some cases I will admit that some retired people are unable to give any more. The issue is not just being on a fixed income but how much of a fixed income.

Friends of mine are both retired. One had been a school teacher for many years. Her husband worked in the New York subway system as a foreman. Their combined retirement income is now greater than $100,000 a year. Their medical expenses are covered 100% by their former employers. This is a pretty nice fixed income for two average people. When asked by their church, they have the ability to be most generous. Most younger workers would welcome the wages of this retired "fixed-income" couple.

Capital Campaigns

Perhaps you have enough challenges just making your annual budget, and then the church roof begins to leak, or the boiler sighs its last breath. Where will you get the $40,000 to solve this problem? Hopefully you have some money in the bank to meet this immediate expense and can borrow from yourself. You might even have to borrow the money quickly from your members. In either case, you must pay the money back. Make your case to the people of your parish and mail out the special roof repair envelopes if the expense is not too great. If you have a lot of repairs that you need to accomplish, you launch a capital campaign. There are many good companies that can help you with this. Good ones let you know the cost of their services up front. It is not cheap, but an excellent, well recommended professional fund-raiser is worth every penny you pay.

A wise pastor who knows little or nothing about conducting a capital campaign will shadow the paid professional and learn how to do this aspect of stewardship. The layman who is the campaign chairman will do the same. In the future, the pastor and layman will be able to conduct additional campaigns foregoing the cost of the professional.

In my home congregation, the pastor wished to do a much-needed refurbishing of the church and its facilities prior to his retiring. He did not want to strap his successor with this large task. Since I was a professional fund-raiser and a member of this church, I said I would donate my time and talents to this task pro bono. He initially felt the cost would be around $300,000 and then raised it to $600,000, which became our campaign goal. The final tab was slightly over a million dollars. This kind of unexpected increase happens in nearly every campaign. Therefore expect the unexpected to happen in your campaign and plan for it. We raised $850,000 in three years and borrowed the manageable remainder.

The remarkable thing was that during the three years of the campaign giving our congregation continued to make its weekly offerings as well. I told our people that there was to be no robbing of Peter to pay Paul. Their pledge was not to come out of their weekly offerings. Prior to the capital campaign we received approximately $400,000 in regular offerings. During the three-year campaign, the members continued to give the $400,000 along with an additional $283,000 a year for the campaign. They had effectively increased their total offerings by 70% each of these three years. Are you impressed? I was. Since the average churchgoer gives less than 2% of his or her income to the Lord each year, there was money available to shape up our church's facilities. We just had to ask for it.

The two pastors of the church and I first made our sacrificial pledge to one another and to the Lord. We then met one-on-one with families blessed with greater wealth and challenged them to give leadership gifts. We scheduled hour-long meetings with the 600 families of our church meeting just eight to ten families at a time. Remember that the smaller the group, the greater the result. We challenged each family to prayerfully consider giving at least an additional $10 each week to the capital campaign. Some could and should give more. We did not ask for identical gifts but for identical sacrifice.

At the conclusion of the meeting, the pledges were made and placed on the altar for dedication the following Sunday. At the meetings, we immediately handed each family 156 envelopes. The three-year period of their pledge began the following Sunday. By doing this, we saved the considerable cost of mailing the envelopes. More importantly, there was no lag time in having the people get into the routine of bringing two offering envelopes to church each Sunday.

We also printed our own envelopes at a great saving. They were not dated, for everyone started and ended their pledge at different times. Those who wanted to give monthly received only 36 envelopes. Those who wanted to give yearly were given three. Those who felt uncomfortable committing to a three-year pledge were told that should they lose their job or come into other hard times, they could stop giving until they got back on their financial feet. When they were able, they would continue fulfilling their pledge. No envelopes needed to be discarded.

Church Endowment Fund

This is the third leg of the stewardship program that every church should have in place. A good stewardship program can be likened to a three-legged stool. One leg is yearly pledges. Another is special gifts to meet occasional needs like putting a new roof on the church. The third leg is end-of-life giving. End-of-life bequests become especially important in order to sustain the life of a church during difficult downturns in church attendance and giving as many churches are now facing.

Most denominations like my own have a pooled endowment fund for the benefit of their churches. They invest the funds professionally for you for an annual cost of about 1% of the principal you invest. Any money realized above the cost of managing the fund is used to support the ministry of the church at large. Your church's endowment fund generates a yearly payout based on a percentage of the amount you invest in it. At this time it is about 4%. The idea is to give your church the benefit of the earnings while keeping the principal intact. For example, if the total of the bequest received by your church is $500,000, your church would receive $20,000 annually in support for your ministry. Sometime in the future your church's very survival may well depend on having endowment income.

Money can be given to your church's endowment fund in many forms and through numerous vehicles. Here are just a few more ways of giving other than cash donations. A house or other tangible property can be left through a will. The church can be made the beneficiary of a life insurance policy. Stocks, bonds, precious metals, and jewelry can be given. The church can be named in a will to receive the residual estate. This constitutes money and things of value that are not designated specifically for named beneficiaries. Oftentimes, the "leftovers" are quite substantial.

There are also financial instruments like charitable gift annuities that someone purchases during one's lifetime. The older a person is at the time of purchasing the annuity, the greater the interest that is paid annually. These annuities can be set up to also pay this interest to the surviving spouse until the surviving spouse dies. The church then receives the money left in the annuity. This is commonly 50% of the initial investment. There are many other investment instruments like this. If someone shows interest, there should be trained people at your denomination's headquarters who can assist you in helping.

Years ago I was helping our local Lutheran high school raise money for a capital campaign. I called on one lady who made a $100 donation. She then asked me if the high school could sell her a charitable gift annuity. She said that she had purchased one recently from the Salvation Army. "I'll have to get back to you," I responded. I contacted someone in my denomination's foundation office, who helped me assist this lady purchase a $50,000 charitable gift annuity naming the high school as the beneficiary.

About a year later, I was playing tennis with the executive director of the high school. He said that the lady had recently died and that the school just received a check for

$48,000. You might think that after my being instrumental in the high school receiving such a large gift, my friend, the executive director, might have allowed me to win our tennis match that morning. It didn't happen, but I had the joy of making it possible for this lady to support the Christian education of our young people.

In the beginning of this book, I spoke of the large number of faithful older people who make up more than half the people in our churches. This is also the group making end-of-life decisions. Today is the day that you should be encouraging them to support their church beyond their lifetimes. In every bulletin and in every newsletter you should print at least a brief paragraph that reads something like this:

First Presbyterian needs your help in ensuring its future ministry. Please include the church in your will. You may want to at least tithe (give 10%) of your estate to the Lord. Remember to include the church's name and address along with the amount of your bequest. Should you wish, the pastor will provide you with the name of a caring and capable lawyer who can assist you.

The Bequest While Living

For years my wife and I had made provision in our wills to leave 10% of our estate to several churches and other Christian charities. The problem was that every five years the list changed in our minds. This necessitated changing our wills to reflect our current thinking. After the third revision, we decided to give the tithe of our estate in a different way. At seventy years old, we decided for the next ten years (statistically one of us should easily reach eighty) that we would donate 1% of our net worth for each of the next ten years. By the end of the tenth year, our tithe of our estate will be complete.

There are several benefits in doing it this way. The charities will get an average of our net worth over the ten-year span. Should we both have a long stay in a nursing home at the end of our lives, our estate could diminish to a degree that our charitable tithe might become very small. This helps to alleviate this possibility. Since we are giving the money away during our lives, no one can contest our actions. Chances are that if we are financially able, the 1% yearly donation of our net worth might well extend beyond our eightieth year thereby increasing our total end-of-life gift.

The benefits to us are great as well. We can decide each year what charities we wish to support. We can direct how a given charity spends our donation at the time the gift is given. Perhaps what is most attractive is that we are able to experience the joy of seeing the good that our sizable donations are accomplishing.

This approach is for the person who has considerable assets and can afford to donate 1% of them each year. This is just one more suggestion that you can lift up to your people for consideration. Some might well find it attractive. Currently 14% of all households in the USA are worth at least one million dollars. For every 100 families in your church, there are potentially fourteen millionaires who could consider this approach to end-of-life giving. Others worth less may find it attractive as well. One percent of each million dollars of a person's net worth results in a donation of $10,000 per year. A gift of this size can have a large impact for good.

Electronic Giving

Increasingly we are becoming a paperless society. Our younger members, as well as some of our older ones, are embracing all kinds of new technologies that have become available. These new giving vehicles, along with paper money and checks, can be used to support your church. Many churches today make online giving available to their members and have this option, along with others, accessible

42

through their websites. It is possible to have your bank regularly send your donation to your church in the same manner it pays your mortgage. Some churches have installed terminals so people can donate through their credit and debit cards. All of these possibilities need to be investigated and at least some implemented in order to make more options available to your people. If someone finds it preferable to give electronically, why shouldn't you provide someone the opportunity? The more options you provide, the more offerings you will receive.

In closing, remember that you can only spend a dollar once. Stretch it to the max and then spend it wisely. Be bold in asking people to support the Lord's ministry at your church. You are not asking in order to enrich your personal wealth, but you are asking people to both sustain and advance the work of the Lord. This is worthy of your time and best effort.

Action Items

1) Discuss ways to change the negative image of asking for money in your church, and then implement them.

2) Visit every line item in your budget, discuss ways savings might be affected, and then act on them.

3) Regularly negotiate lower pricing with all your vendors.

4) Reduce the salaries of paid staff or even reduce your staff if you are spending more than you are receiving annually.

5) Regularly call every person on record and invite them to pray daily for your church and to join you in weekly worship.

6) Ask your pastor to lead small-group stewardship meetings after the model suggested in this chapter.

7) In the next twelve months, conduct a capital campaign to address major repairs and/or additions to your facilities.

8) Launch a church endowment fund, and regularly invite people to remember your church in their wills.

9) Implement or increase electronic giving opportunities for your people.

Three

Invigorate Your Congregation's Worship Life

A Minnesota farmer had a very pessimistic neighbor. When he would greet his neighbor in the morning by saying, "It looks like it's going to be a beautiful day," the neighbor would most likely respond, "I think we're going to have a storm this afternoon." When the sun was out in full force, he would say, "The crops should grow an inch today." The neighbor would counter, "I hope the sun won't dry out the ground." During a much needed rain, the negative neighbor would say that he worried that there might be floods. He was always negative.

Every fall both men enjoyed going duck hunting together. The positive farmer just acquired a new bird dog. It was the best that money could buy. It was trained to do its job beyond perfection. The optimistic farmer couldn't wait to show the dog off to his negative neighbor. With guns and dog they went in their boat to enjoy the hunt. Before long the first duck fell out of the air into the water. The positive neighbor commanded his new dog to go and fetch the bird. The dog immediately jumped out of the boat, walked on top of the water, gently picked up the bird and brought it back into the boat laying it right at its owner's feet. The positive farmer smiled and said to his friend, "Now what do you think of that?" The negative farmer replied, "I bet he can't swim."

You must exhibit a sense of optimism and positive enthusiasm about your church's future even when things appear bleak. Remember I said earlier that admitting the challenges your church faces is the first step in solving them.

Even while doing this, you can still be optimistic and enthusiastic that God will help you meet and solve your problems. Enthusiasm originally referred to someone possessed by God. Possessed by a fervent belief in the power of God, we become a vehicle for God to use in the revitalization of our church.

It is essential we make the worship service an excellent expression of our love for the Lord. "I am not even sure that I would attend my own church," a pastor friend recently told me. "My organist is terrible, and I think that I have the worst choir on Long Island." This pastor is friendly and a very good preacher. Holy Communion is offered every week. God is worshiped and adored. But the poor music ministry at his church is a detriment to his church's growth. At a church I was recently asked to serve as interim pastor, the organist could not even play the Lutheran liturgy. This is big for a pastor serving a liturgical church. He only played three hymns each week, and he did not play them very well. I was told by parishioners that they paid him cheaply. I was happy when he was away, for the substitute was always better. He did have a winning personality, but visitors to this church were tortured by his horrible playing.

If you do not have one, you must find the best available organist and hire this person *yesterday*. A good piano player is even preferable to a poor organist. In most every congregation, there are a few people with the gift of a pleasing voice. Talk to these people individually and encourage them to join the choir. Every week as I process into church and recess out, I am always listening to the voices I pass along the way to see if I am hearing a potential choir member. Your choir must also be the very best that it can be. Some congregations even have a gifted soloist among their members. Use this person's gift regularly. Billy Graham had a wonderful, massive choir singing at his crusades, but his gifted soloist, George Beverly Shea, always sang as well.

Preach to People Where They Are

If you are a pastor reading this book, there is something important that you can definitely control. That is your sermon. I am not a homiletics professor, but I have some definite thoughts on the subject of the sermon after nearly fifty years of preaching. First, it should be no longer than eighteen minutes. Someone researched and found out that this is the maximum length of most people's attention span. Then you should preach to people where they are. Meet them in the kitchens of their lives. One of the best compliments I ever receive from people coming out of church goes something like this, "Thank you, pastor. I thought that you were preaching your sermon today strictly for me."

Preaching from the appointed texts of the day should be your usual practice, but it is not heresy to occasionally choose other texts as the basis of your sermon. If the appointed texts do not evoke a message from me, I look elsewhere. Sometimes I also preach a series of sermons on a particular topic like the Lord's Prayer, Jesus' Sermon on the Mount, or the Heroes of Faith of the Old Testament. God blesses these messages as well.

My sermon is never an eighteen-minute Bible class. I try not to impress anyone by citing Greek and Hebrew words. I try not to allow my theological preparation for the sermon to be regurgitated and eat up any of my eighteen minutes. The sermon is not about me and how educated I might be. It is about what God wishes to say through me to the hurting people sitting in the pews before me. It is about addressing their daily problems and issues with God's reassuring words of grace and love. It is about bringing the listener into a closer relationship with God and speaking God's words of wisdom and truth to their everyday lives. Each sermon should strive to have a "take away." A take away is something that every parishioner remembers throughout the week. By the end of the sermon, the goal is not for the listener to think that

47

the preacher is brilliant but to better understand that God's loving forgiveness is his/hers because of God's grace and mercy.

I also title my sermons every week and list the title in the bulletin for both the current week and for the following week. This does two things. Hopefully it encourages my non-weekly attenders to come more often. It also disciplines me to start my sermon preparation a week in advance. Coming out of church, a parishioner of mine once told me, "I turned down an invitation to play tennis this morning because I did not want to miss your sermon on 'God's Cure for Worry.'"

Recently another clergy member heard me preach. She was a guest of a parishioner. Leaving church, she referred to me as a "contextual" preacher. Honestly, I was not sure whether this was a compliment or a rebuke. Checking into this labeling during the following week, I found it referred to someone's preaching style as one that tried to share the Lord's message in a way that engaged the congregation in the context of where they found themselves. She had me pegged just about right.

In my denomination, clergy are encouraged to chant the liturgy. This is a beautiful thing when the clergy possesses a good or even a pleasing voice. It adds to the worship. When you do not possesses this gift, then do not chant. Excellence should always be the goal of every aspect of worship. I was once called to be the pastor of a very liturgically astute church. When the church's choirmaster told me that the entire liturgy was always chanted in his parish, I told him that chanting was not a talent that I possessed. He responded, "But the rubric states that you will chant the clergy parts of the liturgy." To make my position more emphatically clear, I stated, "I do not care what the rubric states. I'm not going to make an ass of myself in the worship service." When I turned back the call for other reasons, I'm sure the choirmaster felt that his prayers had been answered.

"Pastor thanks for making the First Communion special for the kids this morning by not reading the same thing for each kid." This was a comment of someone who recently attended the First Communion of six beautiful children in the church I presently serve. One at a time, at the beginning of the distribution of the sacrament, I spoke the name of each of the six First Communion recipients and invited them, along with their entire family, to come to the altar to receive the sacrament. After communing each family, I prayed *ex corde* (from the heart) over each of the six children. This was a special moment for each child. Therefore each child was treated specially.

Make Praying Your Strong Suit

I have been privileged to travel to the Holy Land many times. Yael, my favorite guide, told me about one of her pilgrims who prayed at the Western Wall asking God to bless her with children. Until then she had been unable to conceive. It is a custom to write your prayer on a piece of paper, fold it, and tuck it into a crevice in the wall. Literally thousands of prayers are put into this wall, which was a part of the temple of God. Several years after her first trip to the Holy Land, this woman returned. Yael recognized her. She told Yael that she had five children since she first saw her. She was now returning to the Holy Land to ask God to turn off her spigot. She believed strongly in the power of prayer. I do as well.

In my denomination Sunday prayers are prewritten for the liturgist. Each individual petition by the pastor ends something like this, "Lord in your mercy." The congregation then responds, "Hear our prayer." For the most part these prayers are well written and cover many areas of concern. Yet, I would suggest that on some Sundays the pastor write his/her own prayers that address the special needs and concerns of his/her congregation. This will add both variety and vitality to this important part of your worship.

Let me also suggest that each week you pray, by name, for three families in your church. First prepare a mailing envelope addressed to everyone associated with your parish. Choose three at random every week. The week before you pray, using the addressed envelopes you randomly selected, send each family a letter indicating that they will be prayed for during the church service the coming Sunday. Encourage them to be present. List these families in your bulletin the same week you will be praying for them, and also encourage the entire congregation to pray for them during the following week.

As I mentioned earlier, the first thing I asked from every individual of the parish I am currently serving was to pray daily for the church. "As you pray for your family members each day, include your church family as well," I encouraged everyone. I really believe in the power of prayer. Martin Luther was purported to have said that when he faced way too much to do and not enough time to accomplish it, if he did not first spend four hours in prayer, then there was no way that everything would get done. Prayer beckons the presence, power, and guidance of God for your life and for your congregation. It is essential in moving a congregation from surviving to thriving.

God Desires and Deserves Our Worship

Let's make it simple. The question is, "Does God desire and deserve our weekly worship?" The answer is a resounding "yes." Believing this, we do not have to ask ourselves 52 times a year whether we are going to church this Sunday or not. Unless we are ill or have an urgent other commitment, we attend. Going to church is not primarily about meeting our needs. It is about pleasing God who meets our needs every minute of every day.

As we worship God, we are blessed as well. What if someone gave your church a large sum of money with the instruction that for every week for a month each person who attended your church would receive a brand new $100 bill? Does anyone question that attendance would increase for that month? Near the end of the month, after the word got out into the community, there would be standing room only. If you had two services each week, some folks might convince themselves it would be good for their soul to come to both services. Children might even decide to miss Sunday soccer practice to attend church. Every Sunday God gifts us with something infinitely greater than a mere Ben Franklin. We are gifted with his body and his blood for the forgiveness of our sins and the blessing of an eternal life. Why would we want to miss this weekly gift?

Martin Luther was also a parish pastor. One day he visited a member whom he had not seen at mass for some time. Both men sat before the fireplace in the man's living room. Without saying a word, Luther went over to the fireplace and with a pair of tongs, removed one of the glowing, red-hot pieces of wood from the bottom of the fire. He then placed it on the roughly hewn, wooden mantel. As they both watched, the piece removed from the fire quickly went out while all of the others continued to burn brightly. The point was made. We need to be present every week at worship to remain on fire for the Lord. God desires our weekly worship, and we need it.

Other Aspects of Worship to Consider

The announcements are a very important part of your Sunday gathering. Make them at the end of the service when everyone has arrived. Let them become a time to enhance God's mission at your church. I call this important time together

"Moment of Mission." This is a time to motive people to action. It is a time to move from just announcing the mundane to relating the excitement of God in your midst.

Someone once said that it is easier to get away with preaching heresy from the pulpit than to change the order of the worship service. Too many pastors feel that they know the "right" way to conduct worship, and it is their task to reform the worship life of the congregation to which they have been called. These liturgical snobs often drive people away from coming to church. God encounters people's hearts through many forms of worship... even old, outdated ones. Go slowly. Learn to appreciate what is already in place as you seek to help people see the beauty of what might be. After the congregation first grows to love you, they will be more willing to accept change.

Permit me just a few more practical observations and suggestions. Do not change your worship times in the summer. It only will make your attendance less. People are creatures of habit. Changing their worship time in June, then back again in September, causes confusion that leads to fewer people coming to church. The loss is greater than any possible gain. Fewer people attending also results in less money for the church's ministry.

Most churches do not have Sunday school during the summer months. Their choirs go on hiatus. The coffee fellowship hour is stopped. Yet summer is also the time when new families are moving into your community. When these important folks visit your church during the summer, they do not find you at your best. Perhaps you should take another look at this widely held practice of canceling these three elements of your church's life. Invite soloists from the choir to add to your summer worship. People in your congregation who are not part of your regular choir might be able to contribute during the summer. Since fewer children are coming to church, fewer teachers are needed. The summer months are a wonderful time to share the great Bible stories with your children in group settings. It does not take too much to put on a pot of coffee and serve purchased cake. During the summer, less is fine. Cutting these elements out altogether for three months may not be wise.

Remove negative statistics from your bulletin. If your current attendance is usually less than it was a year ago, remove the comparison from the bulletin. Why advertise consistent failure and decline? When things turn around and current attendance exceeds that of a year ago, return these statistics to your bulletin and point out the increase to your congregation. Success breeds more success. Make sure your recessional hymn is one that everyone knows and loves. If people leave smiling, they are more likely to return the following week.

Finally, since the offering is an integral part of the worship service, never just casually stick one offering plate in the middle of the church aisle expecting people to put in their offering as they walk by. Always pass the plate from person to person. When the offering is collected, treat it with respect, lift it up to the Lord in prayer, and place it on the altar. It will not contaminate the Lord's Supper. It will rather be a visible sign of the congregation's gifts of love to the Lord.

Recently, I observed a pastor at a baptismal service simply put the offering plate on a little table in the middle of the center aisle of his church. The pastor made no reference to the offering plate although "Offering" was listed in the bulletin. The service was an hour-long service with Holy Communion. There were about 75 people in attendance. Half of the congregation used the two side aisles, never encountering the offering plate at all. The rest passed the offering plate, and only a very few made an offering. By the offering plate's placement, worshiping God with an offering was deemed unimportant.

I have discovered over the many years of my ministry that very few people who do not attend church services participate in the other parts of the church's ministry. Worship is the hub of ministry. If your church does anything with excellence, let it be the hour you spend together on Sunday mornings. Everything else radiates out from that common experience. More importantly, worship is our weekly offering of thanks and praise to our gracious God. It must be clothed in excellence. God deserves the very best that we are able to offer. Every week we should try, in every way possible, to invigorate the worship life of the congregation we serve.

Action Items

1) Strengthen the music ministry in your church in as many ways as possible.

2) Pastors, every week, strive to make your current sermon your most relevant one yet.

3) Review everything about your Sunday worship life and implement changes that will invigorate every aspect of it.

4) Strengthen your church's prayer life.

5) Regularly encourage and expect weekly worship attendance from your members.

6) Keep your regular service times year round.

7) Retain Sunday school, choir, and coffee hour during the summer months.

Four

Reclaim Your
Inactive Members

"My children have soccer practice on Sunday morning, and I am their coach."

"I work six days a week, and Sunday is the only day I get to sleep in and catch up on my rest."

"I go to church when I feel the need."

"I am a spiritual person, but I no longer believe in going to church."

"Church is boring."

"I'm just too busy."

The above reasons are just a few that I have heard from people who were once active in the church but no longer come regularly. None of them hold water with God. With 168 hours available, if you are too busy to take one hour a week to worship the Lord, you are just too busy.

Most people do not become inactive members all at once. Sure a few got angry at something that happened at their church and left in a huff. But for most, it is a gradual process. They miss one Sunday for whatever reason. This develops into missing several a month. Before too long, they come just on Christmas and Easter. Young people drop out after confirmation or after they leave for college. Parents often follow their children into inactivity. Whole families that were once very much involved become completely uninvolved.

There are some writers who suggest that the smart money almost forgets about inactive members when trying to turn a church around. Getting new members is an easier game, they suggest. One writer stated that it is easier to birth new Christians than to resurrect the dead ones. I am not all too sure this is the case. This has not been my experience. Think about it, the "new" people who some pundits suggest are more reachable are more than likely to be the inactive members in neighboring churches.

God calls us to reach out to the lost... all of them. Begin with the inactive people listed in your own church directory. You even know where they live.

In the first church in which I was the pastor, I took considerable time instructing new members. I met with them for an hour and a half a week for ten weeks. I went over the basic teachings of the Christian faith. I talked about what Lutherans believed. I stressed the importance of regular worship and good stewardship. I introduced them to various opportunities they had to serve the Lord as part of our particular ministry. The more time I spent with them at the beginning of their relationship with our church, the more involved they became. Soon after they joined our church, I also tried to involve them in Bible study and have them grow in their discipleship. In a way, this was preventive maintenance that kept them in good spiritual health and lessened the chance of them becoming inactive.

We are people of habit. The church needs to support and encourage the good habit of weekly worship. This is the reason I stated earlier that it is unwise to even change worship times in the summer. So as soon as we discover that some of our regulars are missing for more than a week, it is important that we call them and inquire about their well-being. This not only exhibits good pastoral care, but it helps to get them back on track. Call it church preventive maintenance or whatever, it works.

Sunday Worship Is Essential — Not Optional

Permit me to further address the subject of weekly worship in this chapter. Too many people have the mistaken idea that going to church is an optional activity for the Christian. It is not. Sure we can have a one-on-one personal relationship with God. This is good. But the Bible also tells of God's relationship with the whole community of believers. This community is the church. In the book of Hebrews, we read that we should not forsake assembling with other believers for worship. The third commandment in Exodus 20:8 (RSV) tells us to "Remember the sabbath day, to keep it holy." First we come to worship because God both desires and deserves our worship. We come to worship because we need to be forgiven and strengthened weekly by receiving Holy Communion. But we also come because we are blessed and are called by God to be a blessing to others in our religious community. We come because other members of our church need us to be there.

Going to worship is not solely about us and our needs. It is about expressing our love and our worship of God. It is about meeting the needs of the others who show up. It is about addressing the needs of our neighbors who live both next door and around the world.

"I can worship God anywhere." There is nothing wrong with this statement as it stands. You should worship God everywhere. Worship is not just an hour-a-week activity but coming together for that hour has never been an optional activity for the Christian. Unlike Mary Poppins who claimed to be practically perfect, churchgoers are not even remotely perfect. The story is told of the couple shopping for the perfect church. At the first one they visited, the people were not too friendly. The next had an uninspiring pastor. The third had terrible hymns. Sitting in the pew of the fourth church, they noticed in the pew card rack something that read, "Are you looking for the perfect church?" Eagerly they pulled it out and read, "If you are looking for the perfect church, please don't join ours, for when you do, it will no longer be perfect."

Faith cannot be faith in isolation. Martin Luther's theology unequivocally states that we meet God in word and sacrament. If to believe means to have Christ present within us, then Luther argues, faith cannot be isolated from worship, for the church service is the place where Christ meets us in word and sacrament. Our faith is a faith that receives. It receives the grace of God through worship. For Luther, absence from the Lord's Supper is turning our backs on and even despising God's precious gift. The church for Luther is the communion of saints gathering in God's presence at worship. Other church reformers like John Calvin joined Luther in this conviction.

The Best Way to
Reach and Encourage Your Members

So how do you reach the inactive members of your congregation whether they come monthly or twice a year, or have completely dropped out? First pray for them daily. Invoke the Holy Spirit to rekindle their desire to attend church. Also discipline yourself to call every member of your parish a minimum of twice a year. When you do this, thank those who are active. Be specific:

- "Thank you for teaching Sunday school. It is so very important to our children's spiritual growth."
- "By your coming to worship every Sunday, you make such a strong witness to our entire church."

For those who are inactive, tell them that God loves them and misses them at worship. Tell them how you miss them as well. Inquire if there is anything that you might do for them or their family. Remind them that both you and the church are there for them. At the end of the conversation, say something like this, "Our worship service is at 10 a.m. Can

I look forward to greeting you this Sunday?" Always try to get a specific commitment from them to come the following Sunday. Many of those you call will have been thinking for some time, "I really need to get back to going to church." Help them move from wishful thinking to concrete action. The sooner you reach out to people who are becoming inactive in your church, the better chance you will have of reclaiming them. Not coming to worship is a habit you need to help them break as soon as possible.

For many of your calls, you will reach only the voice mail. Do not miss this opportunity to also speak words of love and encouragement as suggested above. End every conversation with, "God is looking forward to seeing you at worship this Sunday and so am I. God bless you and your family." Having gone through the entire congregation, return to those whom you missed speaking with personally, and call them a second time.

The beautiful thing about making these calls is that you can usually make ten calls in about one hour. Doing this five days a week yields calls to fifty families. In most congregations, you can call everyone in less than a month. Use bits of time that pop up throughout the day. If I have an evening meeting and the person is late, I make a few calls. There are many small clusters of unproductive minutes available to you every day. Look for them and use them wisely. Of course, the evening hours between six and eight are the most productive times to call. Discipline yourself to make ten calls daily, and your church attendance and offerings will increase. More importantly, you will be effectively reaching and returning people to the Lord.

Making pastoral telephone calls is the first thing I do when I become an interim pastor of a church. It gives me the opportunity to introduce myself to all of the members. For the relatively little time it takes, it always produces good results. I also discover who are the shut-ins who need to be visited monthly. Although these folks can no longer attend church, they become your prayer warriors and will continue to support your ministry financially. They not only need your pastoral care, but they deserve it. They are some of the people who were instrumental in growing your church, and many had been among the most active when they were younger. Never neglect these blessings of God.

Use Email Effectively

Most of your members are not on Facebook or on Twitter, but nearly all of them are on the internet and have an email account. My own mother went online at eighty and continued until she died at 91. Email is a great and inexpensive way to communicate regularly with your people. When I first come to a new church, I ask members to write on the back of their communion cards three things: their name, their telephone number, and their email address. Asking for the telephone number is important, for often the email address they give you is incomplete or illegible. This way you can call them and obtain their correct email address. When you are making your twice yearly telephone calls to every family of your church, use this time to also acquire email addresses you do not have.

Every Thursday I send an email blast to everyone on record in our congregation. I always enthusiastically tell the great things God is doing in our midst. I encourage attendance at upcoming activities like Bible class. And I encourage everyone to attend worship. All of this communication costs nothing. Experts tell us that only about half of the people will actually read your email. Therefore repeating important information every week is necessary. About once a month I also mail church information to those few who do not have an email account. They need to be communicated with as well.

As effective as email is, there is one old communication device that you should resurrect in your ministry. That is the small personal thank-you note. I get six for a dollar at the Dollar Store. I regularly handwrite little thank-you notes to those who do something generous that supports our ministry. This runs the gamut from making a larger donation to serving on the church council. Personally recognizing people keeps them wanting to continue their helpful behavior and makes it less likely for them to join the ranks of the inactive.

Visiting people in their homes is the very best pastoral way to encourage inactive members back into the church. This is especially important if you, the pastor, have done something that has turned them away from the church. Swallow your pride and go. Don't try to explain why you did or said something, cut to the chase say that you are sorry that you offended them and ask for their forgiveness. Let reconciliation begin as quickly as possible. Trying to justify yourself or your actions has little salutary effect.

Around most every church within a ten-mile radius are thousands of people whom the Lord loves and for whom Jesus died. Most are not actively involved in other congregations. These neighbors of ours need the blessings that our church provides. Most of them are family members of ours through baptism. They are brothers and sisters in Christ whom we have yet to meet. In the next chapter we will look at practical and effective ways to reach out to them and invite them to join us and become part of our local family of God.

Action Items

1) Thoroughly instruct prospective new members before having them join your church.

2) Explain often to your congregation why their weekly worship is important to God, to others in your church, and to themselves.

3) Begin calling fifty families a week in your church, commending those who come and encouraging those who don't. Do this twice every year.

4) Collect as many email addresses as possible from your members, and send out a weekly email communication.

5) Buy some "thank-you notes," and send them regularly.

6) Visit those whom you have offended, ask for forgiveness, and invite them back.

Five

Reach the
Unchurched in Your Community

When I arrived at the church that I currently serve, there was no signage indicating the name of the church or its worship times. There was only a small sign indicating the church had a nursery school. That was it. The old, rotting sign had been torn down months earlier. A new two-part sign had been purchased and was being stored inside the church. The $5,000 electronic bottom half was still in the cardboard box in which it had been shipped. There were reasons why this state-of-the-art sign had not been installed... reasons of getting necessary town permits, the coming of winter with its frozen ground, and the like. There are always reasons for not doing something.

But the reasons for getting these signs up as soon as possible were even more compelling. This church had enough funds to only remain open for a few more months. Getting permits could take longer than this. First I went to the local sign maker and purchased an A-frame portable sign and had printed on it the church's name and a big arrow pointing toward the church. Within the field of the large black arrow was the church's "house number" in white. People who might have been wanting to find this church now knew that they had at least arrived at the correct place. It was the beginning, however humble, in reaching the unchurched in our community.

Now we have both our new permanent and electronic sign up and running. We will apply in time for the proper permits.

Perhaps we will have to move our sign in one direction or another to please a local bureaucrat, but as this process was taking place, every day our sign was welcoming thousands of people to join us in worshiping the Lord. I have long ago discovered that it is often easier to get forgiveness than permission.

It is so important that your church sign is in good shape and communicates well. If you need to buy a replacement, just do it. Find out what you need, establish the cost, and ask someone to buy it for you. It makes a good memorial honoring someone. Should you not have one family willing to pick up the entire cost, invite everyone to pitch in. If the new sign costs $2,000, ask twenty people to each give $100 or more.

Less words printed on a church sign are best. If most people see your sign from their car traveling 35 miles per hour past your church, consider placing it so they can read it while traveling in both directions. Put as much information on your sign as can be easily read at 35 miles per hour. Depending on the size of your sign, your church's name, your worship times, and "All Are Welcome" might be the extent of it. Experts tell us that seven seconds is all a person has to read and comprehend your sign. Check out the hundreds of signs you pass by daily, and you will become self-educated by the pros on effective signage.

Steal Good Ideas from Everywhere

Most good ideas have been stolen or gently borrowed. Whenever I am in another church, I am always looking for good ideas. Many years ago I published three volumes of a book titled *Ministry Ideabank*. For years earlier, I was the editor of a monthly newsletter for which clergy members sent me their best ideas from every aspect of their ministry. I collected these and then shared them for free with over 2,000 readers. Donations from my readers covered all costs. The payback for my readers and for me was a constant source of creativity flowing into our ministry.

Keep your eyes open for ideas coming from the secular domain as well. Every piece of "junk mail" you receive and every advertisement you read cost someone much money to design and produce. Since the line item in your budget for "ad agency expenses" most likely does not exist, draw upon the creative money spent by others to bring interest and results to your ministry. Inspired by a full-page ad, I once sent a letter out to my congregation with only print on the very top and bottom of the page. At the top it read, "Listed Below Are the Reasons Not to Attend Church This Sunday": The rest of the page was blank. On the very bottom was written, "Join us for worship at Trinity Lutheran Church." We also included the address and worship times.

While I was visiting a friend in a New York City hospital, a banner hung at the hospital entrance that read, "Amazing Things Are Happening Here." I thought, if I were in this hospital having surgery, I would like to think they could do amazing things to help me. At our churches, amazing things are happening as well. Sins are being forgiven, souls are being cured, and people are being healed for eternal life. We have an amazing God! I have borrowed this slogan more than once and hung it on banners and printed it in copy referring to the things God was doing in the churches I served.

While vacationing in Boston recently, my wife and I visited Old South Church. There I picked up a most creative postcard invitation to this church. On the front was written in scroll like form:

*"Skeptic. Certain. Confident. Fearful. Gay. Straight. Bisexual. Married. Divorced. Single. **JESUS DIDN'T TURN PEOPLE AWAY.** Looking. Partnered. Female. Male. Trans. Saint. Sinner. A little of both. Immigrant. Native. Strong. Weak. Got-it-together. Lifelong screw-up. Long-time member. Just walked in the door. Parent. Child. Housed. Homeless. Believer. Questioner. Questioning be-*

liever. Doubter. Sports junkie. Tree hugger. Geek. **NEI-THER DO WE.** *Cool kid. Loner. Rich. Poor. Just barely making it. Skeptic. Certain. Confident. Fearful.* **Beloved."**
Old South Church in Boston. A place of extravagant welcome since 1669.
Corner of Boylston & Dartmouth St. at Copley T Old-South.org

On the reverse side of the card was the address of the church along with its Facebook address, web address again, and worship times. At the bottom was written: "You are welcome here."

When I returned home, I immediately called this church and asked for permission to use this idea for my home church. The director of communication told me that this would be fine, and as a matter of fact, her church had gotten the idea from a church in Indiana. She even gave me her printer's name. With a few changes, we had professionally printed in color our own glossy postcard. Five thousand pieces only cost us $300.

We made ours slightly smaller so that it could more easily fit into a shirt pocket. On the reverse, we added a line map along with our name, address, telephone number, service times, and our website. Anyone remotely familiar with our area could look at the line map and find us.

On Sunday we clipped three cards together with a slip of suggested instructions to make it easier for our members to share their three cards. Here it is:

Ascension Invitation Card
1. "Do you regularly attend a church in the area?"
2. If No... "Here [hand them the card] I would like to invite you to attend mine."
3. If Yes... "That is wonderful! Here is an idea that you might wish to share with your priest/minister [hand them the card]."

This is Evangelism 101. It was a good place to start with our parishioners. We encouraged people to hand the cards to whomever they encountered throughout the week. The cards were also handed out before Easter when we have our communitywide Easter egg breakfast, egg hunt, and various other children's activities. We give them to customers at our annual yard sale. If you receive a bag of food from our food pantry, a card goes in the bag along with a verbal invitation. Additional cards are available in the narthex of the church to be taken by members and distributed. We also sent two cards, along with our instruction slip above, to every address on record and encouraged the recipient to share them. More than half of those receiving these were inactive members. It was our way of reaching out to these folks as well.

I wish I could tell you that we had to enlarge our sanctuary because of this activity, but a few people did come as a result of it. More importantly we educated our members and challenged them to share their faith in a simple and do-able way. This is called discipleship. Thriving churches have large numbers of their members regularly inviting others to join them at worship. Conduct a survey in your church, and I believe that you will find that the majority of your current attenders had been invited by another person.

Print Versus
Virtual Communication

We were invited by several Lutheran churches in our area to join them in purchasing an expensive ad in our daily newspaper. It was a full-page advertisement. Each participating church had a space about two inches square to communicate its location and the time of its Holy Week services. We declined. Why? Because before Christmas we kicked in about $200 toward the cost of a similar ad that yielded no measurable results for us. I asked several of the churches that participated and not one could point to anyone who attended their services because of either ad. There were no measurable results.

Unfortunately, print ads are both costly and not as effective as they were years ago. The younger generation reads the newspaper less and less. These people get their news online instead. In the current church I serve, because of the tightness of our money, we could only afford $100 to purchase a quarter-page ad welcoming readers to join us for Holy Week and Easter worship. The ad was nicely done, in color, and had artwork and so on. Not one person came as a result of spending $100 of the Lord's money in this manner. On Easter Sunday, when I saw that we had people at worship I had not seen before, I asked during our Mission Moment, "Is anyone in attendance today because you saw our advertisement in _____?" No one indicated he or she came as a result of this ad. This will be $100 we will save in the future. But we did have a family attend our Maundy Thursday service because they looked us up on our website.

We have had reasonable success in promoting our nursery school by mailing 6" by 8" postcards throughout our community. Print your own cards and choose the zip codes you wish to mail to and solicit. It is not cheap, but the number of students recruited by it made it cost effective.

I do not have much to give you on how to better use your website and social media to advance the Lord's work through your church. I am still using a flip phone because I like its small size. In case you are wondering whether or not you should read any further, I am on Facebook and do text my grandchildren from my iPad. There are many books on how to more effectively use social media. Buy and read one. At 71, I am intent on becoming more efficient in using these tools. An excellent website as well as frequent and creative use of social media needs to be put into play in order to reach more of the unchurched for the Lord. This is a good chance for younger, media savvy parishioners to help you achieve these goals. Involve them.

The congregation I serve has a modest website and its own Facebook page. Periodically I have my sermon taped, and we put it on YouTube and on our Facebook page. Interestingly, 75 people hear my sermon when it is preached, but 400 more people view it online. Now that is hardly going viral. Joel Osteen need not worry about the competition. But we are charged with sharing the Word with the world, and it is nice that we are reaching a little more of it in this manner.

Another fine way to promote your church through your website is to take short video clips and post them for the benefit of whoever visits your website. Video some of your parishioners and have them tell why attending your church is so important to them. Include both young and old. Words of welcome are good. Pictures of your activities are better. Video clips may be the best bet.

Some of you may be thinking that this ship has sailed for you. Others may be thinking that you do not have the money. The synod to which I belong, realizing the importance of its churches having an effective website, has set aside $500 for each one of its 192 churches to either start or make more effective websites. This has been in place for over a year. My current church is taking advantage of this free money. We are only the second congregation to do so. Money and age are not the issue... wanting to do it for the Lord's church is. Also investigate what Twitter, Pinterest, LinkedIn, Instagram, Google+ and other social media offerings can do to help you reach the unchurched in your community. There are presently over 200 from which to pick. Choose five, get a group of younger people together and have fun trying to reach as many people as you can for the Lord.

Personally Invite the Neighborhood You Serve

On nice quality 8 1/2" by 11" paper, we are printing our own special invitations, which include information about our church, nursery school, and summer camp. Cutting the regular size piece of paper in half lengthwise produces two invitations that, when folded, measure 5 ½" by 4 ¼" each. On the inside are the name and address of the church with telephone number, website address, a line map directing people to our church, and a welcome letter with basic information like time of worship and the ages of children served by our nursery school and summer camp. The word *Invitation* appears centered on the front of the closed paper.

Every Sunday we also hand each worshiper one *Invitation* handout along with their bulletin. We encourage them to share it with someone during the week. We also give them a printed instruction similar to the one shared earlier for Ascension. I always carry several invitation handouts with me in my suit jacket pocket never knowing when God will present me with an opportunity to share it with someone.

A recent Sunday was a case in point. It was Mother's Day. I gave every mother a small mirror and hairbrush item that flipped closed when not in use. I had 35 of these left over. Every Sunday morning a local Panera Bread store gives its day-old bread to our church, which we then distribute among the members. I decided to take some of these small brushes and give them to the women who had to work at Panera's on Mother's Day. After gifting eight to the store employees, I looked around the dining area and saw it filled with families. I had a dozen of our invitations in my pocket, so I went table-to-table wishing each woman dining with her family Happy Mother's Day while handing her a portable hairbrush with mirror. "This is a gift from Faith Lutheran Church along with an invitation," I repeated a dozen times. Everyone smiled and took both. God had just turned having too many hairbrushes into an opportunity to invite a dozen families to church. Statistically, half were unchurched.

In the town of the parish I currently serve, this year two parades are scheduled to go right past our front door. One is the annual Memorial Day Parade and the other is a special parade celebrating a milestone for our local fire department. We are setting up free coffee and bagels on our front lawn for both our parishioners and our neighbors. Along with me, several of our members plan to cover the entire parade route handing out invitations to our church. We expect to invite over 500 families during these two events alone. The cost to the parish will be around $100. We cannot afford to miss this wonderful opportunity.

A friend of mine and his wife went to McDonald's every morning for years and ordered a Happy Meal™. Over the years they acquired over 2,000 children's toys. His wife passed away, and now he is getting rid of the toys she faithfully collected. As the vicar and I walked the Memorial Day Parade route, we handed each young child a "vintage" McDonald's toy as we said, "A gift from Faith Lutheran Church." At the same time we handed the parents one of our invitations. The gift increased their willingness to consider the invitation piece. Often there are little things collected in your church's closet such as religious pins that someone deemed too good to throw away. Hand these out with your church's invitation. Be creative.

We also hand out our invitations at the local train station just a mile from our church. Seven trains arrive from New York City between six and seven every evening. Meeting them, we hand out invitations to an additional 100 people in an hour. The train station is also a good place to invite your neighbors to your Christmas and Easter services. I invite friendly, outgoing people with a ready smile to help me do this. Young people also are good at this. People are more likely to take something from them.

At least one day a week we go door-to-door and invite the unchurched to join us for worship. Should they not be home, we note the address so we can visit this house at a later time. If they are home or not, we leave our invitation piece. When someone answers the door, after introducing ourselves, we ask for just three minutes of their valuable time. The first question we ask is, "Do you regularly attend a church in the area?" Those who do we commend. Those who don't we invite to Faith while handing them our invitation piece. Then we ask whether they have any children under five living in their home. If they do, we also give them one of our nursery school and summer camp brochures and invite them to consider sending their child. We thank them for their time and wish God's blessings upon them and their family.

Whenever we encounter people who are not our parishioners, we invite them. If you come to a special event like a Baptism, First Communion, or Confirmation at our church, you will be invited. If you have a child in our nursery school or summer camp, you will be invited. If you deliver mail to us, you will be invited. If you walk down the sidewalk in front of our church, you guessed it, you will be invited.

When you meet people anywhere, try to engage them in conversation before inviting them to your church. Recently, I was in the checkout line in the local supermarket. I had planned to hand an invitation to the checkout girl. I noticed that the fellow behind me had eight one-gallon containers of water in his shopping basket. I asked him, "Are they for filling your swimming pool?" He smiled. We chatted a bit; then I handed him one of our invitations. He gladly took it. I also handed one to the checkout girl. It really isn't that hard. Engage people in conversation first and then invite them.

In our Sunday bulletin, we print some effective ways parishioners might share their weekly invitation piece. This not only reminds people to share at least one every week, but it also shows them additional ways that it can be shared. Most importantly, this little practice of encouraging our parishioners to share a weekly invitation piece underlines for all of them that witnessing must be a regular practice in the life of every Christian. Below is our current "Top Ten List" of effective ways to share an invitation.

Effective Ways to Share Faith's Invitation Piece
Top Ten List

10) Post one on the library bulletin board and leave one in the library book when returning it.

9) Share one with Jehovah's Witnesses and Mormons when they visit your home.

8) Offer one to the teller at your bank upon completing a transaction.

7) Hand one to the waiter or waitress at a restaurant along with your tip.

6) Place one on the bulletin board in your supermarket, and share one with your checkout clerk.

5) Share one with someone you meet casually in the bank line or in the beauty parlor.

4) Leave some at the train station with the train schedules.

3) Leave some on the end tables in your doctor's and dentist's offices.

2) Give one to a family member and invite him or her to church with you.

1) Give one to a friend or neighbor and invite that person to come with you to Faith.

A Few Other Important
Things to Consider

On our church's printed mailing envelopes, along with the return address, we have written in the lower left-hand corner, "Sunday worship at 10 a.m." Everyone who receives mail from us, be it a bill payment or a congregational mailing, knows where we are located and the time of our worship.

A neighboring pastor, whose church is also on a major street like ours, had a creative and interesting way of inviting the unchurched into his parish. At his annual church fair and pumpkin sale, he gave whoever wished the opportunity to have their child photographed with Santa Claus. For no cost to the family of the child, the picture was taken. Later a 4" by 6" copy was mailed to them. The pastor collected the address, telephone numbers, and email address from each family. With the picture came an invitation for the child to attend Sunday school and for the family to attend church. Clever and successful.

The founder of the Salvation Army, William Booth, once said that the ringing church bells on Sunday mornings seem to cry out, "Come to church." He then mused that when he twice pounded his bass drum, it encouraged him rather to "Fetch 'em." I strongly believe that if we want our neighbors to enter our churches, we must leave the building and fetch 'em. To encourage their members to do just this, some churches I've seen have signs erected by the exits of their parking lots which read, "You are now entering God's mission field."

In the Lutheran liturgy at the end of the service, the pastor says, "Go in peace. Serve the Lord." Another form goes like this, "Go in peace. Share the good news." Having heard the word of God and having participated in the Holy Sacrament, we are directed to go out and share what we have received with God's people outside of the walls of our churches.

As you witness to all, you might also want to focus on the few. In other words, are there specific subgroups of people in your community whom you could be particularly effective in reaching? In my first congregation, we lived in an area where there were many Roman Catholics. Lutherans and Roman Catholics are in many ways closer together in their theology and worship practices than are Lutherans and some Protestant denominations. I noticed early on that many people coming to my new member classes were former Roman Catholics. Once divorced, Catholics can no longer take Holy Communion in their church unless their marriage is first annulled. Since nearly half of all marriages end in divorce, divorced Roman Catholics formed a subgroup we could easily serve. Some congregations are more welcoming to those who are gay; others reach out to specific ethnic groups such as the Guyanese. Is there a group that you might be better at attracting and serving?

Like everywhere else, satisfied customers are your best salespeople. You need to help those coming to your church to reach out to those who are not. Provide them with inexpensive information pieces to give to those whom they invite. Your newest members are often your best recruiters. Call upon the Holy Spirit to bless these efforts.

As you are reaching out to the unchurched, also be working hard to establish an excellent Sunday school and youth program. Younger families, which most churches desperately need, are looking for both. Staff your church for growth not for dying. You do not hire a youth director when you get enough youth; you hire a youth director in order to attract and to get enough youth.

The Lord's money is to be spent, not to be hoarded. Holding on to your money in order to use it to balance your budget for the next ten years might not be as wise as using it all up in two to three years to see if you can reverse the downward trend of your church.

A healthy church is one in which the faces in the pews look like the faces of your community. Our churches are not fortresses for keeping out the community. Ethnic groups, who increasingly may be becoming your neighbors, need to be especially welcomed into your church. God's church was put there for them as well. Your neighbors surrounding your church are part of your congregation as much as those who come inside. In my home church, we have established a Latino ministry. We have done this because a growing number of our neighbors are Latinos. It is now an active congregation of 75 participants. We have a bilingual deacon leading these members on a part-time basis. We are currently working with a church in a neighboring community to help it establish a Latino ministry as well.

Concluding Thoughts

This parable is told about the early years of our country's history. Many towns along the New England coast experienced ships that wrecked having ventured too close to their rocky shorelines. These towns put together teams of men who braved the rough seas and rescued those whose ships sank. Unfortunately, these occasions were frequent enough that it was decided to set up lifesaving stations along the shore. As the years went by, a dormitory and dining room were added to accommodate those who were both rescuers and rescued. Over the years as the facilities became more elaborate, the men's willingness to courageously risk their lives became less and less. In time no one rowed into the storm to save the dying. Today, this is why swank yacht clubs are all along the coastline of New England.

In many ways, we are all naturally witnesses. If you eat at a new restaurant that is surprisingly good, you tell others of your experience. If you get a deal on a car, you encourage others that is the place to buy a car. If Macy's is selling leather coats for a song, you tell everyone you know. If you are attending a terrific church where you meet God and receive the sacrament and have your sins forgiven, you are reluctant to tell anyone. People especially need to hear about God's life-enhancing love. We need to tell others how God expands the beauty of our lives not lessens it. Our mission is simply to share Jesus Christ with the power of the Holy Spirit. We leave the results in God's hands. Results are God's domain.

When we do not take the opportunity to share our faith or to invite someone to our church, the devil high fives his fellow angels in hell.

Finally and perhaps most importantly, you need to help your people grow beyond Evangelism 101 so that they will feel comfortable verbally sharing their faith with others. Teach them how to write an effective testimony and to share it. Kennedy Evangelism Explosion is just one of many good programs available to help you do this. This does not happen overnight, but it needs to happen. Like Jesus, invite a few people to become your disciples. Teach them. Then remember how Jesus changed the world with just twelve.

Action Items

1) Erect an effective sign in front of your church.

2) Look for and steal good ideas from everywhere and from everyone.

3) Build an effective website.

4) Put your church on Facebook and at least four other social media outlets.

5) Print invitation cards for your church and distribute them in every way possible.

6) Identify those for special focus and then especially reach out to them.

7) Spend money to reach people for the Lord; do not hoard it.

8) Work to have the faces in your pews mirror the faces of your community.

9) Teach your members how to more effectively share their faith.

Six

Remove the
Roadblocks that Impede Thriving

I was having breakfast in a deluxe hotel located on a beautiful lake in Switzerland. Looking out the floor-to-ceiling windows at a 180-degree panorama on a picture-perfect day, I marveled at God's magnificent creation. There were mountains in the distance, and the lake mirrored the few puffy clouds in the sky. It was a pinch yourself, this cannot be real, moment. Then it happened. I spotted it. It was to my far right near the bottom of one window. Bird poop! A bird had flown over recently and let go. My perfect image was ruined. I tried very hard to avoid looking at the bird poop, but try as I might, my eyes kept returning to it. I guess it is part of our imperfect human nature that something nearly perfect can be lessened considerably by even a small blemish.

Arriving at a church where I was filling in for a pastor on vacation, I was surprised at the hesitancy of the usher to allow me to use the pastor's office in order to vest. Entering the office, I immediately understood his reluctance. It was a mess. It was embarrassing to him to have me see it. Paper was strewn all over the desk. There were multiple piles of papers and magazines stacked all over the floor with only a small pathway leading from the office entrance to the desk. Post-it notes were stuck everywhere. They were even attached to the ceiling. If a potential member of this church saw the pastor's office, one might have second thoughts of the effectiveness, if not the sanity, of the spiritual leader. I did.

It does not take very much to turn visitors away from your church. From the minute they arrive, they are evaluating whether or not they will return. Blemishes that they encounter not only lessen their experience but also become roadblocks to their returning. In this chapter, we will look at several different kinds of roadblocks that impede the mission of your church to reach people for Christ.

Whenever you are selling your house, you increase your chances for a successful sale by staging it properly. The grass is cut, flowers are planted in the front yard, and the bushes are neatly trimmed. All debris on your property is removed. The front door is freshly painted. You want the very first impression to be a good one. You clean the inside of your house as well and unclutter it. The bathrooms are especially sanitized of all odors. No dirty dishes are left in the sink.

The house of God needs to be kept spotless as well. Your visitors can be likened to customers. They visit and wonder whether or not they will buy into your community of faith. I have been the supply preacher at dozens of churches and sometimes cannot believe what I encounter... grass uncut, weeds growing everywhere, front doors a mess, garbage all over the property, and sidewalks dangerously broken. All of this leaves a negative impression even before I step into the church.

Once inside, many churches look like a Salvation Army Thrift Store with donated clothes and boxes of other items piled everywhere. The nave of the church is often little better. Pew racks are a mess, the floors are dirty, and cheap plastic flowers adorn the altar. Someone once told me that you can almost tell the health of a congregation by using its restroom. Look at your church through a visitor's eyes, and remove these roadblocks that might keep a person from returning. No visitor has ever been offended by encountering a tidy, well-kept church.

Consider even inviting a local real estate agent to visit your church and suggest ways to increase its salability. Have the agent give this to you in writing on letterhead. It will become more authoritative by doing this. You are selling your church in a way to every visitor and to everyone who passes it on the street. Tell the agents you will mention their kindness and their agency's name in your newsletter as a way of thanking them. This will increase their willingness to come.

Even if you are struggling, work hard to give your church the look of success. At one church I served, money was so tight that we did not have enough paid custodial help to keep the church as clean as we wanted it. We therefore recruited a group of parishioners to clean the church every week. One woman told me how much she enjoyed working in the Lord's house. The serenity she felt working in our quiet and beautiful church made her day. Believe it or not, she even thanked me for the privilege of cleaning the church.

Genuine Friendliness Encourages
Visitors to Return

Most churches consider themselves to be friendly and welcoming. We write the word *Welcome* on our outdoor bulletin boards. But in fact many are not particularly friendly to visitors. Visitors to your church have it tough, for often they come not knowing anyone. This is why they frequently arrive just as the service is beginning. They usually sit in the back of the church in case they wish to make a quick exit. They are uneasy. They can love the sermon and enjoy the music, but if they do not feel welcome and experience some warmth and friendliness during the hour they are with you, they will more than likely not return.

Visitors do not want to be singled out for public attention, asked to stand up, or do anything much more than observe. A warm hello, a nice smile in their direction, and a "please come back" probably is enough. This is most beneficial if it comes from someone besides the pastor.

We are often not good judges of how visitors are treated in our church. Let me suggest that you make an arrangement with a neighboring church to swap worshiping families for just one week. Each family becomes a visitor to the other church. After the service, each family then meets with the pastor and several of the parish leaders to share their experience. The following Sunday both congregations should be informed about what was learned from their special visitors. In general, do everything possible to encourage your visitors to want to return for seconds.

Work Hard to Resolve Conflict

There are many levels of conflict that can destroy the ministry of a church. Conflict will soon drive potential members away, for they already have enough conflict in their lives and do not need to encounter more in the church. I have often said that where there are five Lutherans considering any church matter, you have six opinions. Varying opinions can frequently be healthy in reaching a good decision. Conflict is never helpful. Where there is conflict, there are winners and losers, and then the church as a whole loses.

Several years ago, a noted Lutheran high school headmaster and I were both invited to consult with a large church. On its campus it also ran a K through twelve Lutheran school. We were told that the problem for which we were hired was with the school's principal who was purportedly not doing his job. There was conflict between him and the head pastor. Initially speaking with the pastor, I wondered whether the pastor was using us to help him get rid of an entrenched staff person who had been at his church for many years. We would provide the cover.

As my colleague and I interviewed about fifty staff and leaders of both the church and the school, another scenario evolved. We discovered that an even larger problem was fracturing this church. There were some inadequacies that the principal had, but the pastor and his assistant pastor were an even greater issue. They could not stand one another. Each had developed a core of supporters and had drawn up battle lines. The church was split in two.

Our first recommendation to the church council was that the principal be given a written job description and evaluated every six months. This principal was the kind of person who said yes to everything asked of him. Because of this, he had the time to do very little well and was roundly criticized. We thought he might be reclaimed. Because of our other major recommendation, we felt that the church especially needed him at this particular moment in its history. We recommended that both pastors leave this parish and seek calls elsewhere. Both camps needed to lose their leaders who had allowed personality issues to split the congregation. With both pastors gone, there was a greater possibility of coming together and healing. When we reported this to the church council, I thought we might be attacked, for they strongly loved and supported the head pastor. After much prayer, the council saw the wisdom of our recommendation and worked with both pastors to resolve the major conflict in this church. Within a year, both pastors had calls to other churches.

Be sensitive to where there is friction that might lead to open conflict in your church. There are many conflict resolution resources available to help you. Laypeople reading this book need to work with their pastors in easing tensions in their parishes. Encourage everyone to frequently practice the Christian virtues of love and forgiveness. Recently a woman in my parish rehearsed before me how a pastor from another church angered her. I agreed the pastor had acted wrongly. I then pointed out to her some of his many good traits. I concluded our conversation by saying, "With his thoughtless behavior toward you, he has provided you an opportunity to take the higher ground and forgive him even though he does not deserve it." When we seize such opportunities to be Christ like, conflict in the Body of Christ becomes less likely.

Neglect the Good to
Be Able to Accomplish the Better

Sometimes the good is a roadblock that impedes the better. You have twenty important things that you must accomplish today. Trying to accomplish them all, you find that you do not do any of them particularly well. This is what I suggest that you do. Decide which five of the twenty are most important to fulfilling God's mission for your church. Do these first while neglecting the other fifteen to the glory of God. You read it right. It is God pleasing to neglect the good to be able to accomplish the better.

Is it good to be a member of the local Chamber of Commerce? Sure it is. Is it good to attend a weekly pericope study with neighboring clergy even when the text for the next Sunday almost writes your sermon for you? Sure it is. Is it good to be present for every ladies' group meeting in your church? You betcha. Is it good to be a member of several regional church and local community groups? Why yes! Who will criticize you if you visit hospitalized parishioners daily? Nobody will. Whether you are a pastor to a congregation of a thousand or a hundred, it is easy to fill up your week with meaningful and good activity. You can be doing a lot of good and useful things, and your church will still close. Especially at this time in history when developing a thriving church is most difficult, you need to neglect the many good things you are doing to have more time to do the better things which are more important in ensuring the growth and strengthening of your ministry.

Does this mean taking the time to cut the cost of items in your budget? Yes it does. It is the job of the finance committee, but it is yours as well. It amazes me how many pastors do not even know the size of their church's budget or are not even interested in the amount of their weekly offering. Get interested, for having enough money and spending it well is vital to your church being able to carry out its mission. It means taking the time to make the Sunday morning worship hour the best possible. It means making the telephoning of your inactive members a top priority. It means training and leading your members in ways to invite the unchurched in your community to join your church. It means ditching the good you are doing for the better... all to the glory of God.

Allow me a small aside. When I attended seminary fifty years ago, I was not instructed how to effectively share my faith. Preach and conduct liturgy, yes... share my faith one-on-one, no. I was also not instructed on how to conduct a stewardship program. As I talk with recent graduates of my denomination's seminaries, they may have taken one elective course covering these areas, but their instruction was not much more than mine. Today many seminaries continue to train men and women to be successful pastors in churches in the 1950s. Seeing that I did not possess these important skills either of sharing my faith with a nonbeliever or leading a stewardship effort, I sought to acquire them. Every clergy member must. Today they are especially essential.

Remove the Fear of Failing

The year was 1927. The Yankees were playing the Athletics in Philadelphia. The first two times Babe Ruth came to bat, the Athletics ace, Lefty Grove, struck him out on just six pitches. It was the seventh inning, and the Yankees were at bat. The bases were loaded, and the Athletics were leading by two. As the Babe came to bat, the fans were on their feet screaming. Everyone in the ballpark knew that the great Lefty Grove would strike out the Sultan of Swat for the third time. First pitch, strike one. On the second pitch,

Ruth swung so hard that he fell down. Picking up his pudgy body, he dusted himself off, straightened his cap, and stood in for the next pitch. People present that day said that the third pitch was thrown so fast that they did not even see it. All they heard was the crack of the bat. The ball sailed out of the ballpark over several rows of houses for the longest home run on record. Most everyone knows of Ruth's 714 career home runs. But few people know that he also held the record for striking out. He did this 1,330 times... the most of any player of his era.

If you want to succeed mightily for the Lord, you also need to be willing to fail. Everything you try will not succeed. But if you are willing to step out of your comfort zone and try something risky and hard, many times there will be great results. Do not be afraid to try. You can both succeed and fail to the glory of God. The most successful ministries have an abundance of both.

Not everyone will like you. It took me the first couple of years of my ministry to stop trying to please everyone and be loved by all. Not everyone was going to join my mother in recognizing how wonderful a person I was. I do want people to like me, but it is not the first priority in my ministry. I know of pastors who downplay the ministry of stewardship in their churches because they believed that asking for money is not appreciated by their parishioners. The church that I am now serving, which nearly closed, said that members were not asked to pledge for years. They balanced their budget each year by siphoning $30,000 to $50,000 a year off a $300,000 legacy received a few years earlier.

There are some things you can easily discover not to like about me. I am not perfect, but parts of me are excellent. Rather than internalize and be wounded by people who do not like me, I chose to feel sorry for them, for they have deprived themselves of the enjoyment of the parts of my better nature. In the Old Testament, the prophets of God did not win any popularity contests. Jesus, the perfect Son of God, was impaled on a cross. A pastor friend of mine often said of himself, "I look good on wood."

Every church has its alligators snapping at everything you do. For some of my parishioners, I could do absolutely nothing right. For a few others, I could do nothing wrong. I was more worried about offending my friends than my detractors, for they were the ones I could still disappoint. Thankfully, most people stood in the middle. Do not fear doing what God is calling you to do. You have not been called to be a politician telling people what they want to hear. You were called to be a pastor to tell people what God wants them to hear. You were not called to be popular but to be faithful. Share Jesus Christ in the power of the Holy Spirit and let the chips fall where they may.

General U.S. Grant in many ways was a failure in life. He was a drunk. He was unsuccessful in business. The South's great general, Robert E. Lee, was by far his superior as a tactician. There were several reasons why Grant eventually defeated Lee, but mostly it was because he would not allow himself to be defeated by failure. Generals before him, whom Lee defeated, pulled back after a battle licking their wounds. Grant regrouped and went right back after the famous Southern general. In time he wore Lee down, and the war ended with their meeting at the Appomattox Court House. Things may be difficult and seem almost hopeless, but we need to keep on with God's help doing the best we can with the talents we have. You are not perfect, but I'm sure parts of you are excellent.

Remove the Idols of the Past

"I can remember a time when we had 100 children in Sunday school, and now we have only three."

"We used to have church suppers and a young mother's group. It was so wonderful."

"Once we had three worship services with 500 people attending, and look at us now as we rattle around with just one worship service."

Often the glorification and idolization of the past inject the roadblock of disappointment into the present. There are reasons why our church was larger in the past but is struggling in the present. Lamenting the present and becoming lethargic only make things more difficult. Discourage worshiping the glorious past when it negatively influences the ministry of the present. Things are what they are. Now let's deal with it. God is not dead.

Recently the church I serve celebrated its sixtieth anniversary as a congregation. Pictures depicting large groups of smiling people from their glorious past were placed around church. The handful of charter members still alive were given special attention. "Oh how good the early days were," was heard in different forms throughout the period of celebration. I decided that we should also celebrate what God was doing presently in our midst. Three months after I arrived as interim pastor, it was quite apparent that God was doing some wonderful things for the great benefit of this parish. All projections were that it would survive.

Since this church had literally been reborn and given a new lease on life, I thought it would be good to take a large picture of the "new charter members" of our reborn church. So right after church on the announced Sunday, I gathered all present in the front of the church, or approximately sixty people. In the front row center, we placed a chair on which we seated Grace our 100-year-old member. Next to her stood Claudia, our sweet three-year-old.

The picture was enlarged to 2' by 3' and placed on a stand in our narthex for all to enjoy. On the top we placed a sign which read, "Reborn... Blessed People by God... February 1, 2015." These were the new charter members of our reborn church. The present replaced the past as our new focal point.

We no longer were looking in the rearview mirror to where we had been but rather were looking forward to where God was leading us both in the present and in the future.

Action Items

1) Enhance your church's curb appeal.

2) Spotlessly clean and unclutter all your facilities.

3) Invite a realtor to make suggestions about how to present your church better to the public.

4) Work at ways to increase your friendliness toward visitors.

5) Attempt to stop conflict before it spirals into more destructive behavior.

6) Neglect some of the good things you are presently doing to concentrate on the better things you should be doing.

7) Do not fear failing. Rather fear what might result if you do not try.

8) Remove the idols of the past and replace them with new visions of the present and the future.

Seven

Expect
God's Miracles

My wife and I visited Nova Scotia. During our tour, we stopped at the cemetery where many of the victims of the *Titanic* are buried. When you think of this tragedy, there is no reason that this beautiful ship had to take 1,516 victims down to a watery grave. It happened because of misplaced trust.

When the *Titanic* was out of Queenstown on the third day, it was notified by wire that there were icebergs in its path. The wireless operator took the message and scorned it, because everyone was told that this was an unsinkable ship. Hours later another cable came saying there were icebergs ahead. The wireless operator never wrote it down. After all the *Titanic* was unsinkable.

In an hour a third message came. "Warnings, icebergs are in your path." This time the operator wrote it down, and it was delivered to the captain. He handed it to the director of the White Star Line, which built the ship. He looked at it and threw it in the trash. A fourth warning came, and the captain told his crew to be on the lookout for icebergs. That was all that was done. A fifth warning came at 9:30 p.m., and once again the people did nothing but continue to pursue their eventual demise. Another ship in the area, the *California*, provided a last warning at 11:30 p.m. Shortly thereafter, the lookout saw icebergs. His screams came too late. Collision was inevitable. Even though the iceberg cut a deadly 300-foot gash in the ship's side, there was no worry, for everyone on board believed that the *Titanic* was unsinkable.

There were not even enough lifeboats on the *Titanic* for all of the passengers and crew. There had been no lifeboat drill. In the panic of the moment, many of the existing lifeboats were lowered merely half full. Watching the tragedy unfold, many of the people in the lifeboats later reported that even then they did not believe the *Titanic* would go all the way under. The unsinkable just can't sink.

Can there be a more dramatic example of putting all of our trust in the false promises of the things of this world? Because of doing this, at 2:00 a.m., on April 15, 1912, 1,516 people died. My wife and I paid our respects at their graves in Nova Scotia.

In this book, I have tried to present many ideas and methods by which you can help your church turn the corner from merely a focus on surviving to one of being able to thrive once again. In this chapter, I hope you will more clearly see that it is ultimately God who provides the help and energy we need to secure our future. Yes, gifted pastors and talented laypeople are important instruments of God's grace whom God bestows on our churches. But in the end our hope is not built on "unsinkable ships" but on a loving, powerful, and miraculous God. Now I wish to share with you just a few of the many miracles I have witnessed in the churches I have served. Permit me to brag on God.

The Sidewalk Miracle

Five years ago when its senior pastor retired, I was asked to be the interim pastor of the parish I attended. Two years earlier, I ran the church's capital campaign, and we raised $850,000, or three quarters of the money needed for a major renovation. Nevertheless, we were eventually left with a $300,000 mortgage. But God was not done with us yet. Heading home for lunch one day, I encountered a man standing in front of our church casually looking at it. I greeted him and inquired, "Can I help you?" He told me that he had just eaten lunch in the diner across the street, catty-cornered from our church. He happened to spot the little piece of our church that was visible from his table. Even though he was on his way to inspect another facility, he decided to walk over and take a look. He was the pastor of a church looking for a new home.

I asked about his church's needs. Remarkably, what he needed was exactly what we had. When he would need to use our sanctuary and Sunday school classrooms, they were vacant. I invited him in. He was impressed with our facilities. We both were delighted that God had provided our unexpected encounter.

I asked him what his church might want to contribute for the Sunday and Wednesday night use of our facilities. "We will give you $4,000 a month," he told me. I quickly figured that having his church with us for just five years would enable us to completely pay off our mortgage in record time. Paying off our mortgage early would also save us nearly $200,000 in interest payments.

In a few weeks, we ironed out all the details. I was not only pleased with their generous financial support but was delighted that this fine Christian church was also using our sanctuary to praise and worship God every week. Was this lunchtime encounter on a sidewalk in front of our church just a chance encounter or was it much more? I saw it as one of God's miracles. The other pastor did as well.

The Miracle of the Soup Kitchen Church

I was painting my daughter's shed when my cell phone rang. It was the bishop's assistant. She told me that she needed a coverage pastor for a little African-American church in our community. Its pastor of thirty years had retired. It would only be for fifteen hours a week. Would I be willing to help? After I prayed over this request, God told me to accept it. I thought that fifteen hours a week was quite manageable. And I reasoned that the shed could be completed as well.

It did not take long to discover that this church was in big trouble. The newly retired pastor was suing it for $30,000 in supposed back wages and benefits. It did not have an elected church council. The just-retired pastor had fired the old council and picked one to his liking. This church had merely $2,000 in the bank. The vacated parsonage was a mess. The organist was horrible. You get the picture. But these were all minor compared with the big problem.

For thirty years the members rented their church basement to a soup kitchen, which fed approximately 100 people a day. The church depended heavily on receiving monthly rent money in order to support its ministry. Just as I arrived, I was told of a rat infestation in the basement. As the exterminator took care of the rat problem, he found the basement full of toxic black mold. By law, no one could use the basement until this issue was resolved. What made things even worse was that the church did not have any restroom facilities other than those in the basement.

Having to vacate the basement, the soup kitchen took up residence on the sidewalk outside the church. Volunteers handed out sandwiches from the trunks of their cars. On Monday of each week, they also barbecued a hot lunch for everyone. I signed on to help at the soup kitchen as well. I felt my fund-raising skills were needed on its behalf and in turn for the church's benefit.

The problems of this small church were many and great. Everyone felt it would soon close and be sold... everyone but God! In part, here is what God did. God inspired a retired gentleman to take on the parsonage to clean it out and renovate it. God brought the people together, and they elected a dynamic church council. Church attendance increased dramatically. I discovered the "organist" was better on the piano. I had him play the piano instead. He played for very little pay and was a really nice fellow. We could not afford better. He stayed until the Lord led him to retire early. Thank you God.

In time, the total cost to gut, disinfect, and rebuild the church's kitchen, dining room, three bathrooms, and four classrooms was $115,000. The church was only able to raise $5,000 toward this project taking place in its own basement. Unbelievably, our renter paid the rest. Even more, during the eight-month renovation, the renter also paid $1,000 a month rent to our struggling church. In the middle of this project, a stranger was reading an article about our plight in a small community newspaper. She later told us that she had been looking for a place like ours to help, and her answer and direction were provided by a small article written by one of our volunteers. She wrote a check for $50,000. Subsequently, she gave another $15,000 and told the soup kitchen to call her in the future if we needed help. All of these blessings... coincidence or miracle?

Today under new pastoral leadership this church continues not only to survive but to thrive. Since the soup kitchen was only operating from Monday to Friday, the church began its own new ministry, which is called "Pasta and the Word." Every Saturday it feeds eighty additional guests. Noticing a growing Latino population in the community, this congregation has added a worship service in Spanish. They also provide English as a Second Language class. This was a church with so many problems that everyone, including myself at times, worried it would close. With a big miracle from God, it continues to proclaim the gospel (now in two languages) and help feed the hungry in its midst.

The Miracle of the Atheist

The next three miracles happened in the congregation I currently serve. It needed more than one. In chapter 1, I have partially told their story. During the first month of my ministry there, I was told that the second Sunday in December was traditionally the Sunday school pageant in church. I had only noticed a handful of Sunday school children. But the pageant leader, I discovered, was quite enterprising. With our few children, she added three of her own grandchildren which she recruited from a neighboring church. She drafted two of our 75-year-old men and dressed them as shepherds. They must hold the record for the oldest shepherds ever in a Sunday school pageant, but the pageant was delightful.

During our Moment of Mission, I told the story about how we had cut the costs of our giving envelopes from $1,200 a year to less than half. The grandmother of our three kings came up to me as the service ended and said, "I will give you the money for the envelopes." Enthusiastically, I reacted, "God bless you!" What she said next nearly floored me. "I do not believe in God," she retorted.

She then questioned me, "How much will they cost?" I said five to six hundred dollars depending upon how many we will have to eventually mail to people. She questioned me further, "Then how much shall I give?" Believe it or not, I told my new atheist friend, "Pray about it." That same week she came back to the church and handed my volunteer secretary a check for $1,000. Hearing this, I thought, "Now if God can motivate an atheist to donate $1,000 to this dying church, there is nothing that we cannot accomplish together." Miracle? I believe so. In my entire ministry, I had never had someone tell me he or she was an atheist as that person exited a worship service — and then make a $1,000 donation! This is the stuff of God.

The "Butts in the Pews" Miracle

During our small group "Assuring Faith's Future" meetings, one Saturday morning as we were going into the church to pray, one lady asked me, "Are you looking for a weekly pledge or a one-time gift?" I instinctively answered,

"Yes." We continued the conversation a bit later. She told me, "What we need are more butts in the pews." She was astute and knew that our aging congregation needed younger families and a youth program to attract them. She continued, "I'll make a weekly pledge, and I will also give $20,000 to help us get more people interested in our church." We decided that her gift would be put into a special fund. The following Sunday she gave $5,000 as a down payment on her commitment. We were off.

I wanted to name the fund, "The Butts in the Pews Fund," but thought better of it. We now call it the "Faith Forward Fund." The money has been set aside to be used when the new, permanent pastor arrives. The pastor along with the church council will have the complete say as to how this money will be used to achieve its stated goals. But the story does not end there. We thought that others should be invited to join this endeavor. The exciting part is that this money will not be part of the budget, and its only purpose and use is to help us do evangelism and bring more people to the Lord. This would be desperately needed in order for us to thrive. Together we decided to announce a match for the remaining $15,000 she pledged. She would match other gifts from the congregation two of her dollars for every one additional dollar donated. This already motivated another $7,900 in gifts from the congregation. A friend of mine in Colorado, on hearing this story, generously sent $500 to our Faith Forward Fund.

But the miracle continued. In the middle of a harsh winter, I had finally been able to have lunch with a friend. We were both very busy, for it took us two months to schedule our time together. He was also Lutheran but not from the ELCA. He was a generous supporter of the church to which he belonged. In addition to this, over the years he had given generously to several church projects in which I was involved.

The morning of our meeting, I slipped and fell on the ice in my driveway and split open my forehead above my eyebrow. I should have gotten stitches, but I did not want to cancel because I was stuck in a doctor's office. I put a big bandage over the cut and went to lunch. About every five minutes, I had to mop the blood that trickled down my face.

At lunch my friend asked me about the church I was presently serving. I told him the great things God was accomplishing, especially the "Butts in the Pews Fund" and the $15,000 matching gift that I was promised. I was secretly praying and hoping that he would financially support this ministry as well. Before the end of our lunch together, he simply said, "I'll send you a check." I was thinking he would send $500, maybe $1,000, which would be matched two for one. In about five days, his letter arrived at the church. I nervously opened it. His check was for $15,000. God had seen to it that the original pledge of $20,000 had doubled to over $40,000. Miracle? I think so.

The Miracle of the Heart

The miracle that has been the most impressive has been something that a woman in her late seventies said to me when I called and spoke to her soon after I arrived. I referred to it in an earlier chapter. It merits further magnification. Because her last named starts with the letter W, she was one of the last people I spoke with when I was calling every member of the parish. I told her the problems that we faced and that her church might close in five months sometime around Easter. She responded straight out, "I won't let it close." She was willing to do whatever it took so that this ministry would continue. Not one person in the church wanted it to close, but she was the only one who was willing to commit herself to not letting it close. Her heart and her love for the Lord were that great. For me it was the miracle of the heart.

I believe her witness and conviction were the single most important aspects that God inspired, which turned this ministry completely around. Later when I invited our entire congregation to our "Assuring Faith's Future" meetings, I told the members about this woman's commitment and invited them to join with her and say, "I will not let Faith close." The majority of the church has now united with this woman in her resolve. Its future looks very bright.

What has resulted in just six months? A miracle. Six months ago, this church was barely surviving and was scheduled in the minds of many to close. It did not have enough money to pay either the vicar or me. We both worked pro bono. Thankfully, we were both blessed sufficiently to be able to work in the Lord's vineyard without pay. The church had a projected year-end deficit of $46,000 with approximately $20,000 in the bank to cover it. It had no money to call even a part-time pastor. Today it has a current bank balance of over $170,000. It just passed a $198,000 balanced budget for its next fiscal year. It is currently seeking a full-time pastor and is now able to pay that pastor the full compensation package suggested by the church.

Your church must always reach for something greater that it can achieve. Believe that with God's help, you will be able to attain it. The space between what you are able to do by yourself and what needs to happen in order to thrive is the place of God's miracles.

How many times have I heard someone say words to the effect: "It will take a miracle for our church to survive?" I feel like responding, "Yes, so? God grants miracles." Believing in God, pray for and expect God's miracles in your church. They come in a myriad of ways. In every church I serve, I can hardly wait to see what miraculous surprises God has planned.

Action Items

1) Share stories of miracles you have witnessed in your personal life.

2) Share accounts of miracles God has already given your church.

3) Delineate three miracles currently needed in your ministry.

4) Publicly and expectantly ask God to grant them.

Eight

All Hands on Deck —
Everyone Is Needed

When a ship is foundering and at risk of sinking, all hands are needed on deck. This is not the time to be painting the staterooms or sitting around sharing stories of days gone by when there was smooth sailing. The sinking ship demands the total attention of everyone on board. Everyone must do whatever it takes to first keep it afloat and then help it regain seaworthiness to continue its course and reach its destiny. One might think this would be obvious to foundering churches and their members. Regrettably, often it is not.

Dying churches that are still able to afford a pastor are frequently looking for one possessing a magic wand. Perhaps there is a good fairy God pastor somewhere out there who could wave a magic wand and with one bibbidi-bobbidi-boo, make everything better. These wands are always in short supply. Although every call committee is looking for a pastor who possesses every talent the church needs, these clergy are not in abundance either. But within the membership of your church, God has all that God needs to move it from surviving to thriving.

On January 26, 1905, in South Africa, a Captain Wells discovered a diamond weighing 3,106 carats. After being cut into 530 carats, it was named the Star of Africa #1 and placed in the British Royal Scepter. It is currently displayed among the British Crown Jewels and resides in the Tower of London. The largest blue diamond is the 44-carat Hope Diamond residing in the Smithsonian Institution in Washington DC. In 1969, wanting to display his undying love for his lady, Richard Burton purchased a 69.42-carat, flawless diamond for Elizabeth Taylor. Owning or wearing any of these gems would make anyone feel pretty special. Martin Luther once said that "no greater jewel can adorn our bodies than baptism, for through it we obtain perfect holiness and salvation." We who are baptized are in possession of this wonderful gift of salvation. Therefore wholehearted participation in God's church is not too much to ask from all members of the family of God.

Many seem to forget that at their baptism they became part of the church completely. There are no conditional baptisms. Baptized, you are part of God's family and a member of the team. At a large Christian gathering, I once saw a guy with this printed on the back of his sweatshirt: "The King's Kid." God is our parent in common; we need to recognize we are the king's kid and become God's obedient child.

While in Arusha Tanzania, I visited a local church. The pastor asked the deacon of that church to have an opening prayer. Here is the memorable beginning of his prayer:

God of all creation who gives us this beautiful day and life itself, who hung the stars in the sky, and who also generously provides our daily bread, we welcome you into our presence. Dear Lord, what can I do for you today?

Before he petitioned God for one thing, be it to heal a sick child, to bless him with higher wages, or to even bless his church, he first worshiped God and then he did something wonderful and unique. He asked God to direct his day in God's service. "What can I do for you today?" he prayed. I felt a bit embarrassed, for seldom have I asked God in prayer what God might have in mind for me to do.

Everyone in our church has been given talents by God to do something. Saving the world is God's work, but the Holy Spirit uses our hands. Seeing a problem, we might be inclined to ask, "God why don't you do something?" God answers, "I did, I created you." We need every set of hands on deck. God calls every one of us to be ministers. I often address the people of the church I am serving as, "Fellow Ministers." Through prayer God will direct us when we ask, "What do you want me to do today?" Encourage every one of your baptized members to ask.

A woman at one church I read about was troubled because she could not for the life of her figure out the particular talent that she could offer up to God. She did not possess a good enough voice to praise God through the choir. She was a follower, not a leader. She did not know her Bible well enough to teach it. One day another parishioner casually mentioned to her that she had a beautiful smile. "Could that be my special gift?" she wondered. She decided to arrive at church early every Sunday and greet everyone who came to worship. She then sat in the back pew so that she could be the first one out and thereby wish everyone a wonderful week. She later commented, "I smiled them in, and I smiled them out!"

On one Sunday morning while in Bukoba, Tanzania, I got up early enough to witness the sun rise over Lake Victoria. Making my way down to the lake, I encountered two young Tanzanian men. I greeted them and was happy they also spoke English. After a polite exchange of greetings, I inquired whether they were Christians. With happy faces one proudly announced, "I am a Roman Catholic!" What he said next nearly floored me. He continued, "And I love Jesus very much!" In my lifetime, I have proudly stated that I was a Lutheran. But I never just said casually to another person, "And I love Jesus very much." The Christian church in Tanzania is thriving. This brief encounter showed me just why.

In Conclusion

Most everyone knows that the very first heart transplant was done by a South African surgeon named Dr. Christian Bernard. His eighth heart transplant was done on a man named Lindsey Rich. By a strange coincidence, Mr. Rich's horoscope for that day read, "You may have a change of heart." Someone had to first die for Mr. Rich to have his change of heart. Almighty God sent us Jesus Christ who died for all of us so that we too might have a change of heart and put God first in our lives.

For the true believer, Christianity is more than just a religion; it is a way of life. The first time you were deeply in love, you thought about that person all day long. When you woke up in the morning, they were the first thing on your mind. You went to sleep thinking about them as well. You thought of things that you might do to please them. You loved them and tried to show it in as many ways as possible. Should this not be the way we treat our God? Jesus says in Mark 12:30 RSV: "and you shall love the Lord your God with all your heart, and with all your soul, and with all your mind, and with all your strength."

If this book has provided you with some fresh ideas on how to move your church out of the survival mode into a more thriving ministry, then it has accomplished its purpose. We have discovered that we can expect great things from God, when we are willing to attempt great things for God. First we need to give God our willingness, and then God will accomplish even miracles through us.

Whenever things seem nearly hopeless, remember the great Old Testament story of David fighting Goliath. David was a fair-haired kid maybe five-feet tall. He was a good harp player. Goliath was over nine-feet tall. He was a powerful man and a champion warrior. But Goliath was outmatched in this fight, for David fought him with the power of God on his side. David let the stone fly from his sling, and God directed it to hit Goliath between his eyes... the first guided missile in history. David's God gave him the victory. Victory can be ours as well by daily inviting the power of God to be at our side. As God was with David, God will be with us.

One Final Note

I invite you to share with me the story of things you are doing that are creative and have worked to strengthen your church's ministry. Please email these to me at krahns@msn. com. I will share your ideas with others and also forward to you several of the best ideas I have received from them. Everyone will be blessed.

Action Items

1) Daily remember that you are a blessed member of the family of God through baptism.

2) Every morning ask God, "What can I do for you today?"

3) Let your hands become God's hands.

4) Make your Christianity more than just your religion. Make it a way of life.

5) Tell someone you meet today, "I love Jesus very much."

6) Share your ideas for revitalizing the church by emailing them to me.

About the Author

John Krahn has been a pastor for nearly fifty years. From pastoring the largest multistaffed Lutheran church in New York for 18 years, he currently works with congregations whose very survival is in jeopardy. During his long ministry, he has been the CEO of a Lutheran social service agency, the director of admissions at a Lutheran high school, an Army chaplain, and the owner of his own business. Currently he is an interim pastor and parish consultant in both stewardship and evangelism. He is also a much-published writer.

Krahn holds a master of divinity from Concordia Seminary in St. Louis; a master's degree in Theological Education from Union Seminary, New York; a master of education from Columbia University, New York; and a doctorate in ministry from New York Seminary, New York.